QUEER THEORY, GENDER THEORY

QUEER THEORY, GENDER THEORY

An Instant Primer

RIKI WILCHINS

alyson books
los angeles

Manufactured in the United States of America.

This trade paperback original is published by Alyson Publications,
P.O. Box 4371, Los Angeles, California 90078-4371.
Distribution in the United Kingdom by Turnaround Publisher Services Ltd.,
Unit 3, Olympia Trading Estate, Coburg Road, Wood Green,
London N22 6TZ England.

First edition: August 2004

04 05 06 07 08 **a** 10 9 8 7 6 5 4 3 2 1

ISBN 1-55583-798-0

Library of Congress Cataloging-in-Publication Data
  Wilchins, Riki Anne, 1952–
    Queer theory, gender theory : an instant primer / Riki Wilchins.—1st ed.
    ISBN 1-55583-798-0 (pbk.)
    1. Homosexuality. 2. Bisexuality. 3. Transsexualism. 4. Gender identity.
  5. Postmodernism. I. Title.
  HQ76.25.W55 2004
  306.76'01—DC22   2004046355

Credits
Cover photography from Photodisc Green.
Cover design by Matt Sams.

FOR GMR. YOU ARE MY LIFE.

CONTENTS

ACKNOWLEDGMENTS

I want to thank my Alyson editors, Angela Brown—who had the idea of what this book could look like and the determination to make it happen—and Nick Street—who did the final editing and brought it home. Without your support this book would not have happened.

Thank you to Cheryl Chase for your suggestions and corrections to the chapter on intersexuality.

My heartfelt thanks to Anne Nenneau and John Romary on the GenderPAC board, who have sacrificed and given so much to see gender rights grow, and whose support from the beginning made it possible for me to do this work.

A special thanks to Gina Reiss, whose input and edits on the GenderPAC chapter (and many others) was invaluable, as was her insistence that this book be as accessible and inclusive as possible.

Finally, my deepest thanks to Clare Howell, who has been with me for three books now, and who somehow always manages to make it all come out right. You are a writer's gift.

INTRODUCTION

"Nothing in man—not even his body—is sufficiently stable to serve as the basis for self-recognition or for understanding other men."

—Michel Foucault

This is a book I've been waiting to write for years.

Read My Lips: Sexual Subversion and the End of Gender, which I published in 1997, was the radical autobiography. *GenderQueer: Voices from Beyond the Sexual Binary* was the anthology.

But through it all, I wrote and rewrote versions of this book. I produced three versions, in fact, but none I really liked and none in which I could interest a publisher.

I wanted to write theory and take everything I'd learned over the last 10 years and argue, dissect, and apply it. But theory—in particular, queer theory—had fallen on hard times. It was only interesting to academics and graduate students who enjoyed debating "the signifying practices of the prevailing phallocentric economy, with its inevitable tropes and metaphors of hetero-normativity."

And as queer theory retreated further into academic arcana, it become of increasingly less use to the people who needed it, including psychosexual minorities and activists trying to change society.

I started reading postmodern theory because it captured and explained things I'd felt or suspected all my life, but which I'd never put into words. Language had always felt like a poor tool, one that didn't even begin to capture the ways I felt about the world or the things in my head. There seemed to be two worlds—the real one inside my head, and the other one that I talked about with others. I used to wonder what happened to the million things I felt and thought that I could never say, which knowledge and categories and meaning didn't begin to capture.

At the same time, as much as I loved language, I was puzzled by the naïve faith everyone has in words. They seem to believe that all these named things really exist and that anything that isn't named, somehow doesn't.

Words and names wield enormous power. *Jewish, white, straight, male*—what did these have to do with me. Why was I supposed to be *silent, strong, and masculine?* Why don't big boys cry?

I knew I was different. Although I didn't think much about the gender thing, I knew I was different in a way that I wasn't supposed to be, that made me very sad, and that would land me in a lot of trouble if anyone found out.

And I knew someday people would find out. And, of course, they did.

It was understanding that I could have this very different thing about me, that there were no words for it, and that no one understood it, that made me begin to suspect the hollowness and limitations of what passes for knowledge. Throughout my teens, I would walk the streets around our house at night in an intense adolescent haze, comparing different forms of knowledge—for example, how do Freudian psychology and relativity relate?

Knowledge should be hard and accessible. Except, in a very few instances, it seemed to me more like a net you dropped in the ocean that pulled up some things but left lots of others behind.

Or perhaps that's not quite right either. At Coney Island there used to be a mechanical arcade game. For four quarters you got to manipulate a set of pincers on a crane over a heap of chintzy toy prizes. You won one by successfully picking it up, maneuvering it over to you, and dropping it down a chute.

No matter how much you wanted something, no matter how close to you it was, the only way to pick anything up inside that little glass world was with those pincers.

Knowledge seemed like that. The only way to touch something in the world and manipulate it was with thinking tools. And you didn't know anything about the world except what was communicated to you through those pincers.

One summer I went to a summer camp where no one knew I was Jewish. I was just another boy, until my Jewishness came out.

Then everything changed. I got into fights. I became *the Jewish kid.* For those who had never met a Jew, what I did and said became emblematic: So this is what Jews say and do. It was a very interesting form of knowledge.

When I was in grade school, all my neighbors moved away because a black dentist moved onto our block. He made more money than most of them did, but they worried that it was the beginning of the end for property values if they stayed.

So they left. But we stayed along with an 80-year-old woman across the street who couldn't move. Within a year, all my friends and classmates were black.

As kids, we didn't think much of it. We played together every afternoon after school. Sometimes there were fights, but they were fights between friends, not between races. It wasn't until later that we learned we weren't supposed to like each other. A mutual suspicion sprouted, and a new distance. I began to understand how words like *black* and *white* were powerful.

One night while my parents were away, a group of kids attacked our house. They spray-painted the lawn with the usual obscenities, screamed some choice racial remarks, and left a bundle of burning rags and paper soaked in gasoline burning on our front porch.

Our maid, a black woman from Georgia, went out the door alone armed with a kitchen knife to face them down, but they had left. Within weeks, we had too.

In high school I was struck again by the power of words and their meanings. Saying things like "fairy," "slut," "sissy," and "dyke" could shame kids, start little avalanches of ridicule, even get them ostracized.

Everyone feared being different, even the cool kids. Why was similarity such a good thing?

So I know people find postmodernism impossibly abstract. But for me, it has been a lifesaver that offers common sense and practical suggestions.

The hostility toward difference, the deadly comedy of binary gender, the cascading assertions about my body, and the impossibility of identity: Postmodernism is the set of tools that enables me to navigate my world. Maybe it serves that purpose for *anyone* who is or has felt *different.* The reason I wanted so badly to write this book was to share those tools with someone else.

In fact, this book grew out of a conversation I had with my editor, Angela. She said, "In school I used to know this stuff, but now I hardly use it." I told her this was stuff I used practically every day.

So if you've ever struggled with norms of *masculinity* and *femininity,* if you've ever wondered why you're supposed to fit in, if you don't always feel like a "real man" or a "real woman" or you don't want to take sides in the gay-straight-bisexual wars, if you were ever teased because you "threw like a girl" or were "too much like a boy," if you ever wondered if there's more to you than an adjective list like *bisexual, Jewish, transgender, Asian-American, male,* then this book is for you.

In fact, if you've ever wondered if there might be a different way to be human, this book is for you too.

And if you're that rare reader who never wondered any of these things, don't worry. By the time you finish this book, you will.

1. WOMEN'S RIGHTS

Since this is a theory book, we should begin where all good theory hopes to go before it dies: politics. Queer theory is at heart about politics—things like power and identity, language, and difference.

As good postmodernists (more about this word in a moment), we should be wary of the grand stories we tell ourselves—metanarratives that seem to explain enormously complex events spanning decades.

This is no less true when we try to describe the rise of modern American feminism and the gay rights movement, which touched millions of lives and stretched more than half a century.

Still it seems safe to say that gender rights had its origins in these two earlier civil rights movements, and they in turn find their roots in the mother of all such movements: black civil rights.

For it is in the black civil rights movement of the 1950s and 1960s that the familiar tools of modern civil rights movements—extensive grassroots mobilization, ongoing litigation, media management, professional management, political advocacy, demonstrations, and nonviolent protest -- all come together for the first time. This particular configuration worked so well, in fact, that it has become a template for most of the civil rights movements that have followed.

In a way, it should be unnecessary to advocate for gender rights today, because gender was at the very core of the feminist struggle that transformed male-female social relations in the late 20th century. It is difficult today to appreciate just how different things used to be.

I remember a heated disagreement that happened when I was in the fifth grade over whether girls should be allowed to wear pants to school. This was a time when girls didn't grow up to go into politics, practice medicine, work construction jobs, become soldiers, or play rock and roll. Nor did they jog, play basketball, or (gasp!) pump iron.

Women were heterosexual homemakers, and by common agreement they were considered socially and psychologically incomplete until they had a man to marry, bear children with, and make a home for. Men worked, and women kept house, raised families, and deferred to men. Every female over the age of 25 was expected to wear a bra, girdle, hose, and heels when she went out in public.

For their part, men didn't take out the garbage, help do laundry, change diapers, or do the dishes. Come to think of it, maybe not that much has changed. In any case, men certainly didn't take time between jobs to be "house husbands," explore their "feminine sides," or aspire to be "sensitive." There was no crisis of masculinity; there was just masculinity.

Forty years of feminist agitation has transformed much of what has evolved over that time. Women can have careers outside the home if they wish, enter management jobs, become jocks, dress comfortably, and build independent lives.

While much work remains to be done, many of feminism's "radical" assertions about equal pay, women's health care, domestic violence, a woman's right to choose, and participation in sports are now accepted on both the right and the left as common sense.

But this progress did not come without a price. Arguments like "equal pay for equal work" or "equal health care for women" were difficult to dispute—playing as they did on most Americans' basic sense of fairness.

But if they couldn't attack the message, social conservatives did the next best thing: They sometimes attacked the messenger. This kind of thing still works—you can hear Rush Limbaugh denounce not just feminist arguments, but those nasty "femi-nazis."

Feminists were portrayed as angry, humorless, domineering, strident, and aggressive—in a word, *butch*. They just wanted to be men, or even worse, some them of really *were* men.

If the word "dyke" was never actually mentioned, it was always there, unspoken, in the background: a warning to every woman to let her know just how hard she could press her arguments before she, and not her argument, became the issue.

"Mannish" was something no woman wanted to risk becoming, and something no man wanted his woman, let alone his wife, to be.

Conservatives riffed on the common fear that addressing inequality between the sexes would mean demolishing sex roles. Men would become womanish, women mannish. The sexes would become virtually indistinguishable, and life as we know it would cease.

This sort of logical absurdism was most apparent during feminism's greatest fight: the Equal Rights Amendment. This legislation would simply have made equality between men and women a part of the Constitution and is such a commonsensical proposition that I still have to pinch myself to remember it didn't pass.

One of the most effective weapons trained on the ERA was the assertion that it would legally mandate the erasure of gender differences between men and women and mandate the establishment of such things as unisex bathrooms. Such genderphobic arguments generated an enormous amount of traction in those days and—Ally McBeals's infamous unisex toilet aside—would probably still do so today.

If attacking women's rights wasn't always effective, ad hominem attacks on the women demanding those rights was. Feminists were forced to press their political agenda on one hand while fending off genderist attacks on their personal lives on the other.

Which is another way of saying that gender rights were not part of their political agenda. Feminism had focused on winning for women the same rights as men in terms of access to opportunity, pay, and so on, but not the right to masculinity itself. This was not a problem of "separate but equal" so much as "different but equal."

Actually, as we've seen, plenty of the rights sought by feminists involved things that were considered masculine: entering management jobs, playing sports, not wearing girdles, and dressing in pants.

However, the argument was not that women had the right to masculinity, but rather that such activities were not intrinsically masculine, and in any case women could do them *and still be feminine*. This established the gender ground rules under which much of mainstream feminism (but not lesbian-feminism) has continued to operate: Women could do anything men could do and still retain their femininity. Womanhood and femininity were still entwined in this particular set of assertions. Women's femininity was offered as the guarantor that feminism wouldn't go too far. *Too far*, in this case, meant going after gender.

If *separate but equal* wouldn't work because it always implied inequality, would *different but equal* work any better? To a large extent, it has worked remarkably well. And, in any case, the question was largely irrelevant.

America had no interest in tearing down traditional gender roles. Even if feminism had gone after them, it is far from clear that such an attack would have worked, as early gay rights activists were soon to find out.

This notion of how each of us must look, act, and dress because of our sex is deeply embedded in our society. It is the third rail of civil rights: Attack anything except what I often refer to as *primary gender*. In legal terms, it is called "gender expression and identity."

There has been some confusion between "gender expression" and "gender identity." *Gender expression* refers to the manifestation of an individual's fundamental sense of being masculine or feminine through clothing, behavior, grooming, etc.

Gender identity refers to the inner sense most of us have of being either male or female. The term has its origins in psychiatry (Gender Identity Disorder). It is most commonly used to refer to transsexual and transgender individuals, who are those most at risk for feeling some discordance between their bodies and that inner sense.

Few people today would look askance at a highly paid woman CEO with all the trappings of corporate power and privilege. These are structural shifts in our culture, signs of the elimination of cultural barriers to fairness and equality.

But if it's finally acceptable for women to have "masculine" jobs, wield "masculine" power, and achieve in "masculine sports," it is still totally unacceptable for women to *be* masculine. Show the same people a woman with a crew-cut, wearing a suit and tie, and smoking a pipe—in effect, with all the *interpersonal* symbols of gender power and privilege—and they will probably be shocked, disgusted, or at least turned off.

Women in suits and ties or men in dresses still make us profoundly uncomfortable. Attacks by cultural conservatives on our right to gender identity and expression work precisely because they provoke this deep-seated "ick factor." Much like gay people who are welcome to *be* gay, as long as they don't *act* gay by "flaunting" it by public—camping it up, holding hands, or discussing their sex lives—we often want to confer equality without being confronted by it.

As cultural conservatives denounced feminist organizations for being run by lesbians, advancing the *homosexual agenda,* and eliminating all sexual differences, pressure on feminists to distance themselves from anything radical increased.

American culture has always had a fine streak of anxious ambivalence about gender differences. Every few years there is another convulsive effort to anchor such differences in Nature, and convince ourselves that they are an inescapable fact.

The New York Times will cite the latest university study. *Time* and *Newsweek* will run cover stories on "The New Differences Between Boys and Girls," and CNN devoted a 10-minute segment to the topic.

In between there are spasmodic campaigns to soothe our fear that these inevitable, "natural" differences might slip away in the night, courtesy of some villain-of-the-month: feminism, gay rights, single-parent homes, sex changes, or hormones in the food supply.

Such attacks were not against homosexuality per se—whom feminists slept with and what they did in bed weren't at issue. On the contrary, the attacks were intended to play directly on the public's fears about male and female roles, and they worked.

In 1968, the National Organization for Women went so far as to purge any member who was or was suspected of being lesbian or bisexual. While NOW's ban only lasted a year, there was more than a grain of truth in the conservatives' attacks, and predictably the organization's upper ranks were decimated.

Lesbian feminists, on the other hand, have generally been more supportive of women's masculine gender expression, especially within the ranks of lesbian separatists. At the same time, lesbian feminism has sometimes adopted the worst of separatism: a reflexive antagonism toward anything male as well as a tendency to ground womanhood in the most rudimentary biological determinism. This has sometimes made lesbian feminists automatically hostile toward transgender people. And it is especially true in academia.

Lesbian feminist and "radical feminist" academics have a long and ignoble history of labeling transgender men and woman as examples of everything from wrongheadedness and false consciousness to artificiality and patriarchy gone wild.

This has finally begun to change, thanks to the rise of transgender rights and queer theory. However, it is not uncommon for some lesbian feminists to be quietly uncomfortable with FTMs for abandoning the community by imitating men and with MTFs for invading it by imitating women.

The hostility of some lesbian feminist academics is an indicator of how close to the bone the gender issue hits. One lesbian told me, "I'm not a man. I don't want to be mistaken for a man, and I don't' want to be around women who were men." Another commented, "I really love my trans friends, but they also make me sad. We used to have a whole butch community here, and now they're all coming out as men. A whole generation of butches is being lost."

For the most part, mainstream feminist groups have continued to reflect the greater culture's deep ambivalence about gender, remaining largely silent about butch/femme couples, cross-dressers, transsexuals, and intersexuals.

In some ways, this discomfort is easy to understand. However, if you scratch the surface of sexism and misogyny, you almost always find gender. This is apparent not only in our society's astonishing fear and loathing around issues of femininity and vulnerability, but also in the fact that in a male-centered culture, women will always be the "queer sex."

With this in mind, it's fair to ask whether feminism will ever fully conquer sexism without directly addressing women's right to masculinity, gender expression, and identity. "Revisiting gender as gender rights," as former NOW president and GenderPAC cochair Patricia Ireland says, "is a natural next step for feminism. Gender stereotypes lie at the root of so many problems feminists still face."

On the other hand, feminism has produced a whole literature of tough, provocative thought about gender's impact on everything from public spaces to private health. The explosion of feminist scholarship has provided robust alternatives to conventional thinking about reason and language. It has also refocused our attention on social "outsiders" whose voices often go unheard in traditional discourse. In this way, feminist scholars cleared the way for postmodern gender theory, which mined many of the same issues.

In fact, some of postmodernism's most subversive (and popular) critiques have come from feminist academics writing from within that hybrid of feminist and postmodern thought known as "queer theory."

2. GAY RIGHTS

Following right on feminism's heels was another movement that would be inextricably intertwined with issues of gender: gay rights.

In the 1950s Harry Hay, one of America's foremost gay pioneers and activists, spent more than two years trying to find just four other gay men in New York City willing to meet privately to discuss his ideas. A meeting of more than two homosexuals was illegal at that time. The era was so repressive that shortly after Hay founded the Mattachine Society in Los Angeles in 1950, he was kicked out of his own group for being a Communist—and then kicked out of the Communist Party (along with his wife) for being gay.

Actually, no one was *gay.* The word was not yet in popular use. All there was were *ho moh-sek-chew-alls,* a word that in the mouths of some conservatives sounded like it had about 10 syllables.

What few homos there were fell into one of two camps: avowed or militant. An avowed homosexual was any gay person who refused to publicly deny he was gay. Forget about announcing your sexual preference. Any public figure who admitted to being gay, even under direct media questioning, immediately became an avowed homosexual. Militant homosexuals were even worse. They insisted on being open about their orientation. And in the 1950s and 1960s, they were few and far between.

Even into the 1970s and 1980s, announcing your sexual preference, public displays of affection (PDAs), wearing gay pride buttons, mentioning your lover, and challenging antigay laws could all get you labeled militant. In the lingo of the time, you were shoving your homosexuality into people's faces. Things were so bad that even Liberace, a talented pianist hidden beneath an outlandishly foppish stage act that made Elton John look austere—and whose homosexuality was an open public joke for more than three decades-- dared not admit to being gay.

There was no debate about gays in the military. And had there been one, it would not have been "don't ask, don't tell, and don't pursue" but more likely "don't kill, don't dissect, and don't devour."

When the first gay lobbyist dared to appear on Capitol Hill, all most people could think of in connection with gayness was sex. There was widespread astonishment that a grown man was willing to make the rounds of his nation's capital while effectively admitting publicly that he enjoyed fellatio and anal sex. At the time, few people in the gay community expected their advocates to be very successful. The most anyone hoped for was a little much-needed publicity and some visibility for their issues.

It is a measure of the success of gay activists that issues of sex and gender have largely disappeared from the debate on gay rights. Instead, even conservative Republicans have come to frame their homophobia in terms of "special rights," sexual orientation (when it's about whom you want but not what you want to do with that individual), and something obliquely referred to as a "lifestyle."

It was impossible for gay activism to avoid gender stereotypes, for two important reasons. First was the moral reason. By common agreement, the modern gay rights movement began at the Stonewall Inn, when Third-World drag queens and transpeople of color rioted against the NYPD police during one of the cops' routine rousts of gay bars. Moreover, in 1969, butch-femme couples, effeminate gay men, and drag queens had for decades been the public face a closeted community showed to a hostile straight world.

As "visible queers," they had been the ones who couldn't hide, whom everyone, classmates and coworkers alike, *just knew* were gay. Many of them had the scars to show for it. So there were debts to pay.

There was a clear moral imperative for the new gay movement to put issues of gender front and center.

> Gay advocates have been extremely effective in their advocacy for the right to be "honest and open" about who they "really are," though they often confine expression to the bedroom, not to how they look, act, or dress in public.
>
> This is like asking for the right to *be* gay, but not the right to *look* or *act* gay. As a Lesbian Avenger told me, "I not only want my right to be a lesbian but to look like a dyke."

Second, there was a practical reason to address gender. At some time in their lives, probably as many as one third of gay people transcend gender norms in ways that lead others to perceive them *as* gay. In part, this is because gender is a language of symbols. Straight couples can locate all the feminine symbolic content of their relationship in the woman and the masculine symbolic content in the man. But gay couples don't have that option.

In acts of sex—a man going down on his partner, a lesbian penetrating her lover—one partner will be inevitably negotiate symbolic meanings usually associated with the other sex. We can see a similar symbolic fluidity in queer courtship. A traditional butch might signal her sexuality through any number of masculine symbols: short hair, muscular arms, a gravelly voice, a sport coat, flat shoes or boots, aggressive body posture, heavy jewelry, or lots of direct eye contact.

This does *not* mean that in a lesbian couple one partner must be masculine or butch or "the husband." It means that in the shifting give-and-take of romance and sex, one partner will employ the signs and symbolic language—acts, posture, stance, dress—of masculinity. For this reason, gayness and gender will always be inextricably intertwined.

> Masculine symbols aren't *necessarily* masculine. One of the paradoxes of language is that most signs don't have to have any particu-

> lar meaning. For instance, there is no necessary connection between
> the word "red" and the color we perceive as red.

For that matter, homosexuality itself is the most profound transgression of the primary rule of gender: Girls sleep with boys, and
boys sleep with girls. So from a practical standpoint, it is difficult—
if not impossible—for gay activists to pursue the right to their sexual orientation without engaging issues of gender.

For a while, gender was part of the gay agenda. Many early gay
activists intuitively understood that gender was linked to gayness in
important ways. Yet early gay activists, like early feminists, were also
gender-baited by cultural conservatives. *Your women look like men.
Your men act like women.*

Once again, conservatives attacked the messenger as a way to
discredit the message. And as with the women's movement, such
attacks played directly on Americans' fears of a breakdown in traditional gender roles. In the 1970s and 1980s, Americans were pre-
pared to debate some degree of rights for gays, but they were actively
hostile toward anything that smacked of genderqueerness. Mannish
women and effeminate men remained as unpalatable as ever to
mainstream America. At the time, I was involved in a gay rights community group in Cleveland that had its first chance to be on local
TV. The first issue was who would represent us. The natural choice
was Melissa, who had done much of the heavy lifting to get us
where we were. But Melissa also was a big, bad dyke—plaid shirt
and all. And we knew she would not go over with a mainstream
Ohio audience seeing their very first *acknowledged les-bee-un.*

While I'm proud to say that we eventually chose Melissa, our
struggle was a microcosm of what the gay rights movement as a whole
was going through. Activists who were responsible for much of the
success and recognition of the early movement—folks like Melissa,
Radical Faeries like Harry Hay, and transsexuals like Stonewall
survivor Sylvia Rivera—were quickly becoming an embarrassment to
their own movement.

The gender-baiting of gay activists by cultural conservatives produced the same reaction it had among feminists. The "new gay" had to look more palatable and more gender-normative. Gay rights activists began backing away from issues of gender, and therefore from queerness. Gender would slip from the movement's political agenda and disappear until its reemergence nearly 25 years later, when it could be safely isolated as the problem of yet another minority—transgender people, a.k.a. transpeople.

Rather than defend drag queens, fairies, and effeminate men, gay men responded by playing feverishly against type. "Macho gay" emerged as the new look, complete with the emphasis on the gym culture's hypermuscularity that persists today.

It was obvious to many lesbians that this animosity toward effeminate gay men drew from the same well of misogyny that fed hatred of women. This made things very difficult for lesbians. On one hand, they were passionately committed to a feminism that was still deeply ambivalent about them. On the other, they usually found that gay men didn't "get it" when it came to the obvious connection between homophobia and sexism.

For many lesbian activists, this meant having to choose between one movement and the other, or splitting their energies. Many lesbians simply broke off and put their efforts into small, committed groups dedicated to developing a coherent lesbian feminism. Isolated from the mainstream as well as from progressive movements, such groups often developed radical separatist agendas that continue to influence much of feminist theory and activism.

To this day, gender is no longer discussed as a gay issue. You can search the Web sites of every national gay organization without finding butch/fem, drag, or effeminacy mentioned. Gender as a gay issue has vanished from civil discourse. Thus gender has become, in effect, the new gay—it is not mentioned in polite company.

Gay rights activists have responded to conservatives' attacks by stressing the normality of homosexuals. *We're just like straight people, we just sleep with the same sex.* This strategy has been enormously successful. It just happens to be based on false assumptions. This has left the gay community with its share of internalized genderphobia.

It is not uncommon to see gay personals that read "straight looking and acting only" or "no butches need reply." Flaming queens, stone butches, and nellie fairies are still a topic of discomfort. For many gay men, gender is yet another closet to come out of.

I see this in my work. When I speak before groups of young gay men, they are at great pains to show how much they accept me, and how comfortable they are discussing *my* gender issues.

I often disappoint them by asking about *their* gender issues. *They* don't have issues with gender. All the men they know are as hunky as Vin Diesel, and all the women are as feminine as Britney Spears. They don't own Barbra Streisand albums, watch Bette Davis movies, know who Stephen Sondheim is, or have the slightest interest in clothing, haircuts, or hot new home-decorating design items.

So I ask them to participate in a little experiment. "How many men in this room are gay?" Every hand in the room goes up.

"How many men in this room are bottoms?" Every hand in the room goes down. Very quickly. Then they all look around at each other and break out laughing.

"So, you *do* have issues with gender. Either that or everyone in this room is going to stay celibate until at least one self-identified sissy moves into this city."

Then we have a great discussion about *their* gender issues, including why it would be so humiliating for a man to admit that, once in a great while, he plays catcher instead of pitcher.

This is very loaded stuff. It usually turns out that the reason it's so humiliating is that playing catcher is seen as feminine—the woman's role. It also usually turns out that even the buffest guys were once taunted in school or had to *butch it up* at work. What is interesting to me is that this discussion, which is so obviously necessary, has been so long postponed among men who are otherwise sophisticated and aware.

I was once giving a GenderPAC presentation to an L.A. power couple. They said very little, and I had a feeling that I was not connecting. As they waited patiently for me to finish, they were expressionless and quiet. Then the most interesting thing happened.

One man turned to the other and said, "This explains why I always felt so humiliated when mom used to make me hold her purse at the counter in front of everyone while she searched for change."

The other replied, "That's nothing. I used to cut gym class whenever we had baseball because the other guys made fun of me for throwing 'like a girl.'"

They had this entire conversation with one another, as if I wasn't there. These were two very sophisticated guys who were totally out, socially active, and had been lovers for years. Yet there was a huge portion of their lives that they had never once discussed with each other that was still a significant source of shame.

Sometimes, doing gender activism feels like doing therapy. Almost all of us have stories like those described by the couple, but because gender is such a personal thing, we think our experience reflects our own personal shortcomings. We were ridiculed for being a geek or a fag or for throwing "like a girl," or we were too aggressive and athletic or too old to be a tomboy.

When these things happened, we assumed the problem was *us*, not the gender system. We kept it to ourselves and we felt shamed. Because gender expression has never been framed differently, that it ought to be a civil right, never occurred to us.

Making gender a rights issue gives people permission to own how *each of us* is punished for not conforming to gender roles and stereotypes. You give them permission to be all that they are, regardless of whether other people consider them gender-acceptable. It is now acceptable to be gay, but it's still not yet okay to be a fag. You can be a lesbian, but not a dyke.

Yet there is no clamor from gay or feminist activists for an assault against gender intolerance. In fact, there is mostly indifference. Whatever interest exists is carefully confined to transgender people, as if gender only affected the small minority of people who want to change their bodies or genders. Inclusion of transgender people excuses everyone from having to look at the larger gender issues of gays or feminists.

I suspect these are two reasons for this avoidance. First, transcending gender norms is still an issue of personal shame. Not mastering your gender is like not mastering toilet training. If people can't tell if you're a boy or a girl, they feel uncomfortable and/or angry, and you feel humiliated and embarrassed. Second, the successes of both movements have involved distinguishing what we "want" from who we are. *Our issues may be radical, but we aren't.* We're average, mainstream people like you. We're not so very different.

But that doesn't work with gender. Crossing gender lines is by definition *about* difference. Gender rights advocacy is about the right to be different.

When I leave Washington and go home to South Beach, I often unintentionally do several different gender roles in a day. In the morning I often dress in a tight spandex outfit and whisk around on Rollerblades—and get amused whistles from the Cuban men who see me as a babe. Afternoons find me banging bodies with the boys on the basketball court and being called "he." And evenings I walk arm in arm with my lover—a couple of lesbians in our best and most androgynous Banana Republic summer menswear.

I used to complain to my lover that I felt weird, like a failure, being seen in these different ways. Her advice? "You're finally using *all* your voices."

I doubt we can ever hope to really cure homophobia or sexism if we avoid discussing gender. As the head of the *Ms.* Foundation, Marie Wilson, once told me, "Gender stereotypes—that's the basis for all of this."

3. TRANSGENDER RIGHTS

As we've seen, women's and gay rights advocates made phenomenal mainstream progress in the 1970s and 1980s, in part by detouring around some of the more difficult aspects of gender rights. But in the 1990s, gender advocacy received an incredible infusion of energy from two sources: the unexpected rise of an energetic transgender rights movement, and the amazing conquest of academia by postmodernism, particularly queer theory. Both movements would make enormous strides in the struggle for gender rights, and both would pull up short of the goal for very different reasons.

Transcending gender stereotypes had always been a subtext for gay rights. As we learned in the previous chapter, in many ways, gender defined what most Americans thought of when they said "queer." If it is true that queers who transcended gender norms were not well-served by two movements that wanted to focus only on sex and sexual orientation, it was also true that the tremendous political success of both movements held out hope for a better day.

Genderqueer gays and feminists undertook major movement roles, often remaining quietly behind the scenes and hoping for better days. But in the early 1990s that equation began to break down in unexpected ways. A lesbian feminist friend, responding tartly to some new and loud demands for the inclusion of transgender people remarked to me, "Where were all these transgender people in the '70s and '80s?"

I replied, "Oh, they were here. They were just still *gay.*"

Transgender people had always been around, living under the broad umbrella of the gay community. But as gayness and gender became separated, a new term was needed—*transgender.*

In many communities of color, transpeople still simply called themselves *gay*—which makes sense, since white American culture tends to be one of the few that splits sexual orientation from gender. In fact, in many countries, the word *transgender* is hardly used, as is also the case in some communities in the United States. As queer ethnographer David Valentine notes, a black femme-queen who "walks the balls" as part of the New York house culture (and who takes hormones and has breast implants) is more likely to describe herself as gay or queer than transgender.

But gay rights advocates had left cross-dressers, transsexuals, drag queens, intersexuals, and stone butches with battles left to fight. They could love being queer, but could they look and act queer? The answer was still no.

The groundwork for the coming "transgender revolution" was laid by the community's quietest members—cross-dressers. An immense social network of cross-dressers had been forming since Virginia Prince's efforts in the 1960s. Thinking that perhaps what she did was not a perversion, she placed a small ad in an out-of-the-way publication to invite others to join her anonymously in a hotel room.

Twelve men showed up, each carrying a bag or suitcase with women's clothing. There, almost frantic with shame, anxiety, and fear, they all agreed to put on their clothes in front of one another. As a friend put it, "Virginia Prince made it possible for two cross-dressers to look one another in the eye."

By the 1970s, there was at least one major cross-dressing convention each year where men could go for a whole weekend and be themselves, dress openly, and—as long as they didn't leave the grounds—pretend that they were normal and society was tolerant. By the 1990s, there were one or two major conventions a month. And transsexuals began to show up in increasing numbers.

For transsexuals in the 1970s and 1980s, the most important

thing in the world was passing. If you couldn't pass, you couldn't live, and that's still too often true today. Buying groceries, using a lavatory, seeing a movie, or going to class were all incredibly difficult if you were obviously transgender. Finding a date or a mate was practically impossible. It was enough to make you feel like a complete closeted freak—a certain recipe for self-loathing.

As hospitals backed out of the sex-reassignment business, private doctors around the country took it over. It became more democratic: cheaper and easier to get. By the end of the 1990s, postoperative transsexuals probably numbered more than 50,000.

Surrounded by scores of transsexuals and hundreds of cross-dressers at conventions, it was impossible for differently gendered people to feel the same shame. And it was impossible for them not to want to take this strange feeling of being open and unafraid and make it a daily thing. Transsexuals and cross-dressers began to see themselves less as social problems and more as the next oppressed minority. It was a powerful moment of political recognition.

The emergence of the internet and e-mail enabled transgender people to communicate privately and cheaply and to build more elaborate social networks.

I remember trying to put publish *In Your Face,* one of the earliest transgender political publications, in 1995. There was no way to get transgender news, since gay and mainstream media didn't cover it, and transgender publications remained strictly apolitical. I had to call every activist I knew and ask "What's happening in your state?" and then tape and transcribe their answers. Five years later, we would surf the Net to round up gender news."

For the first time, transsexuals became conscious of themselves not as just a social minority, but as a political minority. Enthusiasm for activism, even protest, began to develop. For the first time, there were street actions by transsexual groups such as Transgender Nation and Transexual Menace.

The murder of Brandon Teena (memorialized in the movie *Boys*

Don't Cry and *The Brandon Teena Story*) radicalized many transsexual activists and provided a rallying cry. On the opening day of the trial of Brandon's murderers, 40 people—most of them strangers—flew to Nebraska from around the country to hold a vigil in front of the courthouse. Most of them wore Transexual Menace T-shirts. It was a cultural clash across any number of boundaries. Townspeople saw weirdos—outside agitators—who weren't welcome. School kids came by to gawk. The sheriff's office, largely responsible for Brandon's death in the first place, tried hard to accommodate and protect us.

Around the lunch hour the local neo-Nazis came by in their pick-ups. They spat out their windows, gave "*sieg heil*" salutes, and tried to sideswipe us as they drove past. This was all closely watched by a young aspiring film student, very boyish and muscled, named Kimberly Pierce.

The very idea of public transsexual activism was an oxymoron—it was all about passing as *real,* wasn't it? But from then on, few transsexuals would die violently without a vigil to commemorate their murder.

By 1996, gay newspapers finally began covering transsexual protests, hate crimes, and police violence—topics the press had previously ignored. By 2002, a National Day of Remembrance (which had originated with a 1998 vigil in San Francisco) for such victims was being held in cities around the country. This was the birth of real awareness of the need for a gender rights movement, and the seeds were sown for what would later become GenderPAC.

The push by gay organizations to add the "T" to "LGB" was on for real. An energetic and often rancorous debate over the inclusion of transgender people broke out across the country virtually overnight. Change began to happen very fast. Within two years, LLEGO (the national Latina/o gay group) and the National Gay and Lesbian Task Force both added transgender to their mission statements. A furious battle broke out between transgender activists and the Human Rights Campaign over the inclusion of gender protections in the Employment Non-Discrimination Act (ENDA).

The first National Gender Lobby Day was held on Capitol Hill. American Airlines became the first major corporation to add gender identity to its Equal Employment Opportunity (EEO) policies. Cities and municipalities began passing local ordinances adding gender expression and identity to their nondiscrimination protections. Within seven years, almost every major and regional gay group identified itself or its mission as "lesbian, gay, bisexual, *and transgender.*"

Meanwhile, 55 cities, and municipalities—including the states of Minnesota and Rhode Island—passed gender rights legislation. Behind most of these laws was a handful of determined transsexual activists who had pushed, pulled, and prodded for action, often with the support of local gay groups (but seldom with the help of local feminist organizations).

In addition, 15 Fortune 500 corporations—including blue chip companies such as Intel, Apple, Nike, and IBM—added the gender protections pioneered by American Airlines. Many did so at the urging of a handful of active transsexual and transgender employees working with an internal gay employee group. And, once again, employee groups for women were seldom seen or heard from on the issue, although it intimately affected their constituency.

I blush to admit that in 1995 I was picketing the Human Rights Campaign, and found myself in a meeting where I was yelling at ENDA author Chai Feldblum and HRC Executive Director Elizabeth Birch. By 2000, HRC added gender expression and identity to its mission statement, and by 2003, Chai was kicking off GenderPAC's annual GenderLAW Institute. Elizabeth Birch hosted one of GenderPAC's best fund-raisers, and HRC and other coalition partners moved decisively to add gender language to ENDA.

GenderPAC and HRC began a new partnership to secure congressional signatories on a combined Diversity Pledge affirming that congresspeople did not discriminate based on gender identity or expression. In many ways much of the battle was over.

Yet the embrace of "T" by LGB groups remains far from complete. For one thing, although transsexuals have been historically sheltered in the gay community and have made incredible contributions to the cause of gay rights, the relationship between gender identity and sexual orientation remains murky for many gays and lesbians. Transsexual activists have often addressed this by calling attention to butches, drag queens, and effeminate gay men and pointing out that "It's all about gender, honey."

Yet, because most drag and butch people still identify as gay rather than transgender, some LGB activists remain sympathetic but unconvinced. While they include transsexuals in the scope of their activism, they still see gender identity and sexual orientation as two different, if related, problems.

In addition, the term *transgender* is still burdened with its share of hurdles. It arose in the mid 1990s as a way to distinguish people who cross sexes by changing their bodies (transsexual) from people who cross genders by changing their clothing, behavior, and grooming (transgender).

Within a few years, *transgender* became an umbrella term for *anyone* who crossed gender lines. But (in my own simplistic binary) there is a strong and a weak version of this solution. The strong version includes practically everyone, since almost every person rubs up against narrow gender roles at some point in their lives. In the weak version, transgender not only includes transsexuals and cross-dressers, but also butch/femmes, "aggressive" women, drag queens and kings, effeminate gay men, intersexuals, and so on. The idea is that all people who are *visibly queer* face common political problems and make natural allies.

The challenges are many. For one thing, subgroups such as drag people, effeminate gay men, and stone butches do not perceive themselves as political minorities. They tend to be underorganized and underrepresented politically. Second, for most people, crossing gender lines is still a source of shame, and not something to be claimed, especially as a basis for identity. Witness my room full of gay men who were abashed by the notion that any of them are bottoms. It's hard to rally people to a cause with which they're embarrassed to be associated.

Obviously, most people still don't grasp gender as a valid civil rights issue like sexual orientation, race, or sex.

What has emerged out of the weak version is not a movement of *genderqueers,* but a vibrant and energized transgender movement that is populated mostly by transsexual activists. They have succeeded heroically at passing local nondiscrimination laws and expanding corporate EEO policies. Many have done incredible educational work to raise community awareness. Practically every such advance comes because a few angry transsexuals patiently, boldly, and often argumentatively push the issue forward.

At the same time, *transgender rights* have increasingly come to mean *transsexual rights.* Much of the remaining advocacy in the transcommunity has focused on hate crimes against transsexuals, access to hormones and surgery, name-change laws, insurance reimbursement, and changes to birth certificates. These are all important and often neglected problems. But they are of interest mostly to people who want to change sexes.

Most of the people who might call themselves *transgender* have so far failed to claim the identity, and it's unclear that they will ever do so. It is also debatable whether such people are really included in this new movement, or simply added on as an afterthought. The great "silent majority" of those who do call themselves transgender continues to be cross-dressers, and they are seldom heard from. There may be 100,000 or so transsexuals in the United States, but there are undoubtedly several million cross-dressers, many of whom are married middle-class fathers and grandfathers.

Many cross-dressers have a sophisticated appreciation of advocacy politics, are aware of transgender activism, and have the financial means to participate at a high level. Moreover, they are an underserved community who are bitterly oppressed for something as simple as claiming their feminine feelings and enjoying wearing feminine clothing—something my mom has done for years without noticeable harm.

Cross-dressers should be an enormous source of strength and support for a transgender movement. Yet they are not. For one thing, nearly everyone, even those belonging to other minorities, still con-

RIKI WILCHINS

siders a man in a dress to be a joke. Even many transsexuals look down on cross-dressers because what they do is seen as a choice. As one transsexual said, "I do this 24/7. I can't take off who I am and hang it in the closet on weekdays when it becomes inconvenient."

Yet a man who wears a dress in public—unless he passes really well—is almost certain to be verbally or even physically assaulted. He may lose his job and—if he does not confine his cross-dressing to weekends at distant conferences—his wife and family too. Which is to say, we can make all the jokes we want, but it still takes a real man to wear a dress.

Another complication is that, for many cross-dressers, what they do is also plainly a source of sexual pleasure, even if this is seldom discussed. While gay activists have sought greater legitimacy by deemphasizing gender transgression, transgender activists have sought greater legitimacy by deemphasizing sexual orientation. They sense correctly that changing sexes or genders will be seen as less legitimate and worthy of social recognition if it in any way connects with sexuality and sexual expression.

The upshot is this, even with the rise of transgender activism and its growing success is that gender rights remains a contested frontier. This is strange at a time when *The New York Times* reports that nearly one in seven new cases filed at the Equal Employment Opportunity Commission (EEOC) is male-on-male gender harassment: men calling each other "bitch," "she," or "honey," simulated sex acts, limp-wristed imitations of effeminacy, or sexual menacing. In short, grown men continue to use all the nasty tricks boys learn in high school to humiliate the geeky kid who likes math more than football or girls.

Feminists remain largely unsure what to make of transgender people. FTM transsexuals are simply confusing—they seem to be women who've given up the battle against patriarchy and joined the other side. And while imitation may be the sincerest form of flattery, many feminists suspect that MTF transsexuals and cross-dressers are merely pretending to be women—enacting a parody of sexism's worst excesses in makeup, high heels, and inevitably prodigious breasts.

As for LGB groups, adding the T to your mission statement or political efforts is now considered de rigueur—LGBT is here to stay. Most groups that start out narrowly identity-based stay that way. The fact that the gay movement has opened to politically include both bisexual *and* transgender folks over the last decade is a great testimony to the depth and heart of the gay community.

Yet in embracing the "T," gays, lesbians, and bisexuals still confine issues of gender to the transgender community. This combines the political correctness of the inclusion of transgender people with practical separation from the social and political embarrassments of gender issues. "Gender issues are something *those people over there* have. We're doing the right thing by including them, but it's not a problem *any of us* have."

Meanwhile, transgender activists have lately begun stressing that they include anyone who is *gender-variant* or *gender-nonconforming.* Will these labels bring anyone new to the cause? They're more likely to function as political descriptions than as personal identities anyone is going to claim ("Mom, I'm...I'm...gender-variant"). And few people are likely to rally to a movement in which they're mostly "less subversive" second-class citizens.

If it sounds like I'm disappointed, I am. It was second-class treatment from the gay and feminist movements that propelled many of us to start a separate transgender activism. Now even the transgender movement is creating its own class of politically marginalized people. At one time, we gratefully welcomed anyone who wanted to identify as *transgender,* which seems to me the way it should be. But with new legitimacy came a strengthening sense of identity. I remember when a butch friend first told me she was "only small-t transgender," as if we needed a fresh hierarchy between us.

I began to hear the stories of people being told they weren't "really" transgender because they didn't want to take hormones or have surgery. It would have once seemed unbelievable, but *transgender*—that grand experimental umbrella for all the other misfits— has become yet another identity with its own boundaries, hierarchies, and norms.

The new reverse-hierarchy is forming around who is *most transgressive* and therefore *least privileged*. As one friend put it, "Transsexuals should come first, because they're the most oppressed."

Like many movements, this one is in danger of being increasingly fractured by internal discrimination. In the push to valorize *transgender,* its intersections with age, race, class and disability are increasingly overlooked.

Perhaps the only people who still consistently use the old umbrella as it was intended are queer youth. They call anything *trans* that strikes them as genderqueer.

To some degree, queer youth and queer adults are now speaking different languages when it comes to gender. To a middle-aged white lesbian working at the Michigan Womyn's Music Festival, *trans* summons up an FTM who is taking testosterone. To the 18-year-old she's evicting from the festival for being *trans,* it might mean being a *boy-identified dyke,* one who still identifies as lesbian but not necessarily female.

Transsexuals face a unique array of institutional inequities in medicine, legal identity, insurance, child custody laws, and sex-change laws. It may be that transsexuals are such a singular case that it will take a movement focused solely on their needs to get the job done. As anyone can attest who has sat through the story of Brandon Teena in *Boys Don't Cry,* that would be no small achievement.

At the same time, it's important to bear in mind what GenderPAC intern Seth Goldman once wrote in a passionate—if tormented—e-mail:

Whether in my philosophy of race and gender course at school, in queer circles where transgender issues are trendy or, in the large number of media outlets now covering gay rights, sexual harassment, and women's issues, I'm getting more and more angry that no one will ever say those two words: "gender stereotypes."

I find myself wanting to stand and shake everyone, yelling "It's gender stereotypes—don't you get it? It's right in front of your face!"

Of course I don't, Riki. I do my best to quietly explain. But it's frustrating because I constantly feel that wall in almost everyone's head—whether they're gay or straight, trans or feminist, elder or youth—to seeing the larger gender paradigm that includes them all.

4. DERRIDA AND THE POLITICS OF MEANING

"For [Foucault], Western thought since Descartes has assumed the innocence of reason."

"The art of appropriating the universal was the main business of the Enlightenment."

Mark Poster, *Critical Theory and Poststructuralism*

"The philosophical tradition, at least from Plato on, has always favored the concept of the same; i.e., the aim of philosophical thought has been to reveal the essential characteristics that two things hold in common."

John McGowan, *Postmodernism and Its Critics*

If the political visibility of gender issues was to get its first big boost from the rise of transgender activism, then the emergence of postmodern gender theory was to give it its second.

To understand what *postmodernism* is, or why it was necessary, it is first useful to understand what is meant by *modernism*.

One of the main overarching stories (meta-narratives) that we tell ourselves as a society is that we are a culture defined by truth and guided by knowledge and science.

Like that 1960s T-shirt (EVERY DAY, IN EVERY WAY, I'M GETTING BETTER AND BETTER), for hundreds of years we've been telling ourselves that we are on a continuous upward spiral. This story is what we mean by modernism. With its unquestioning faith in knowledge and progress—and knowledge *as* progress—it is so fundamental to how we think that it appears independent of us, as if it just appeared without pedigree or point of origin.

What would be the alternative? To bask passively in our own ignorance, or to return to a God-centered approach, in which the world exists only in the mind of a deity and can never be known with any clarity?

From the modernist perspective, we must solve the problem presented by bodies, genders, and desires that transgress through more and better knowledge. And that's pretty much the way we've handled it. For more than a 100 years, doctors, academicians, psychiatrists, and researchers have all had their turn poking, prodding, and publishing. Yet after all the diagnoses, experiments, and books, we are still no closer to understanding than before.

In fact, this scientific vigor has only served to politicize the more profound transgressors, solidifying their status as social pariahs while producing little in the way of useful knowledge. The problem such individuals pose is not a consequence of insufficient knowledge, to be solved with more and better science. Instead, we need a new approach, a postmodern one.

The roots of postmodernism—and much of what has become "queer theory"—lie in an obscure 1965 speech given at Johns Hopkins University by a then equally obscure French philosopher named Jacques Derrida. He was so complex, so profound, so *deep,* that even philosophers who heard him, men who read Sartre like you and I read *Doonesbury,* had no idea what he was saying. Gifted with a tremendous and insubordinate intellect, Derrida was also unmatched for chutzpah. He used this speech to announce the end of modernism.

Not much of an finale for a worldview that had dominated the 500 years since the Enlightenment. Derrida's exact words, apparently taken from a speech he had just given in L.A. were: "Modernism is just, like, you know...so *over, dude.*"

Derrida proclaimed that we had entered the era of the "postmodern." And he launched a fundamental critique of traditional Western thought that still reverberates today. Such a sweeping reevaluation of the prevailing social code was largely controversial, and it is still being argued—often heatedly—in *The New York Times* and *The New Republic,* in college introductory classes on "the classics," in graduate feminism studies, on CNN, and of course on Fox News.

A QUESTION OF LANGUAGE

"Everyday language" is not innocent or neutral. It is the language of Western metaphysics, and it carries within it...presuppositions of all types."

"Philosophy plays out only part of what [language] makes possible."

John McGowan, *Postmodernism and Its Critics*

Derrida based his attack in contexts that were particularly useful for thinking about gender and queerness: language, reason, and meaning. Gender is a *language, a system of meanings and symbols, along with the rules, privileges, and punishments pertaining to their use—for power and sexuality (masculinity and femininity, strength and vulnerability, action and passivity, dominance and weakness).* Since it is a system of meanings, gender can be applied to almost anything. For example, in Romance languages like French and Spanish, planes and pencils are masculine, bowls and boats are feminine.

According to Derrida, language has some built-in problems. For one thing, it tends to name whatever is common and shared among members of a speech community. Which is another way of saying that language favors the *Same,* and what is unique, unrepeatable, and private tends to go unnamed.

One of the things about us that can be most private and unique and difficult to repeat is our sense of our bodies—how we feel in them, and how we experience our sense of gender. This means language is already likely to be a blunt tool when it comes to gender. But the problem runs even deeper.

It is not just language that tends to make space for some things while excluding others. It is that words and meaning actually work because of a process of exclusion.

Take "chair" for example. We know the meaning of *chair* by learning what is *not* chair. In other words, we exclude all the other close matches that aren't quite chairs: stools, chaise longues, love seats, and so on. We create the template for *chair* by a process of exclusion. This means that from its inception, the meaning of *chair* depends on all those excluded things that are *not-chair*.

With gender, we create the meaning of *woman* by excluding everything that is non-Woman, and vice versa for Man. We form idealized templates for what is perfectly masculine or perfectly feminine by excluding whatever doesn't fit: the queer, the different, the mixed—people like me.

But because the meaning of Man depends on excluding what is not-Man—what is Woman—it is also permanently unstable. It always operates under tension, under the threat of these exclusions.

This is one reason for today's so-called "crisis in masculinity." The meanings of male-ness and female-ness—never as absolute as they have been presented—have begun shifting rapidly in new and unfamiliar ways. Woman now carry guns, work construction, and get muscular by pumping iron.

To restabilize the binary, we shift the boundaries of meaning and re-erect them. Women in uniform become sexy-spunky, muscles are strong but still feminine, and a sweaty female worker is tough but still very much a lady at home.

It's interesting to note just how many ads for women athletes concentrate on showing them with blow-dried hair and wearing makeup and high heels. The WNBA has been one of the chief offenders here. Some of its butch stars have complained openly about having to pose yearly in pinup publicity photos. These are intended to take the edge off female athleticism and reestablish women athletes as feminine first, athletes second. It's a message to mothers of young fans: *They have muscles, but they're not dykes.*

We expend a tremendous amount of cultural energy keeping gendered meanings intact as well as continually policing, moving, and redesigning them.

The exclusions of language are not limited to separating boy-from-girl meanings. We must also ensure that any bodies that might *queer the act*, by contaminating and combining meanings, are excluded. This can include butches, effeminate men, transsexuals, soft gay boys, intersexuals, drag people, cross-dressers, and other fellow travelers.

SEEING THROUGH TRANSPARENCY

We like to think that language names the real world, that basically the world is *out there* and words just describe it.

We believe language is *transparent*. Like a pane of flat, clean glass, we imagine it conveys a clear and accurate representation of the world beyond without distortion.

But is this true when it comes to gender? A man who glories in his masculinity is *virile, manly, masculine, macho, studly, hunky, two-fisted, stout-hearted, red-blooded, game,* and *gutsy.* A man who enjoys his femininity is *effeminate, effete,* and *unmanly; a fairy, pansy, fop,* or *a sissy.* Colloquially he's a *queen* and a *faggot,* or—in the perennial favorite parlance of locker-room bullies, football coaches, and drill sergeants—*a pussy.*

A feminine woman is *womanly* and *ladylike.* She can even be *girlish* or *matronly.*

A woman who embraces her masculinity is *unwomanly* and *mannish.* Colloquially she's *a bull-dagger, a ballbuster, a dyke,* or simply *a bitch.* About the only way she can be strong and feminine simultaneously is by adding sex to the mix, in which case she's *vixenish.*

We have more words that insultingly describe men who are feminine for the same reason that we fear and hate a man in a dress more than a woman in a suit: His transgression is more of an affront to the politics of gender and therefore more threatening.

More words are required to precisely target the missing aspect manhood—manner, dress, sexual orientation, disposition. Ridicule is more of a success than we realize.

Tellingly there is not a single word for people who don't fit gender norms that is positive, affirming, and complimentary. There is not even a word that is neutral. Because all our language affords are strings of insults, it is impossible to talk about someone who is brave enough to rebel against gender stereotypes without ridiculing or humiliating them at the same time. Language works against you. It is meant to, because the language of gender is highly political.

This application of symbol and meaning can be painful when it's applied to people's bodies. For instance, I'm thinking here of two people I know from the LGBT community. One is a tall, muscular man with body hair who feels that he's really gentle and feminine inside. The other is a lesbian who is curvaceous, petite, and large-breasted who sees herself as smart, butch, and aggressive. The problem is that male, large, muscular, and hairy means masculine and hard, in the same way that petite, female, curvaceous, and large-breasted mean feminine, soft, receptive, and sensual. This *fascism of meaning* is a kind of crime—an assault of meaning that forces people to live as gendered impossibilities.

LANGUAGE AS THE REAL

Derrida pointed out that Western thought has always overvalued or *privileged* language—so much so that we mistake language for the Real. What is named is real, and what is not has no existence.

For Derrida, our naïve belief in language is the flip side of an essentially selfish need to believe in a world that is real, present, and completely available to us at all times. We want to have, as the Bible says, "the Word made flesh," something we can have dominion over.

The idea that the world might be beyond us is rude, frustrating, and even frightening.

The privileging of language as the arbiter of reality has been especially hard on gender. As we've seen, most nonnormative experiences of gender are excluded from language, and what little language we have for gender transcendence is defamatory. Moreover, all aspects of gender that are not named are also assumed not to exist—to be make-believe.

This obliviousness is not limited to transsexuals, cross-dressers, butches, and drag queens, all of whom are perceived not as *doing a gender* but rather as *imitating a gender*. It also impacts a lot of other people as well. For example, while my partner has a female-ish body, she tends toward Banana Republic menswear (but recently bought her first skirt in two decades) and is often mistaken for a young boy. Her relationship with me doesn't exactly qualify her as either a lesbian or a heterosexual. Romantically, she is comfortable as a butch or a femme, a top or a bottom, and all the things in between.

We have no name for this kind of gender. Whatever my partner is, it is assumed not to exist. It is silenced. She, in fact, is often silenced when she tries to explain herself to others. She is denied the words with which to tell her story, to communicate something as basic and fundamental as "This is who I am, this is how I see myself, and this is how I want *you* to see *me*."

Whatever gender she is doing, it is assumed to be derivative of the real, named genders (a boyish girl or something similar). She is described in terms of what she is not. Description becomes an act of replacement and erasure.

This is even more true for the newer and more radical genders that youth are starting to explore, such as boy-chicks (boy-ish or boy-identified), no-ho tranny boys (no-hormones), faggot-identified dykes, andros (androgynous gendered), trykes (transsexual dykes), and bio-femmes (feminine biological female). To be an unwomanly woman or an unmanly man requires an act of rebellion, a willingness to fly in the face of language, reason, and meaning.

Derrida's willingness to denounce language's obvious harms

means maybe we're not crazy, alone, or impossible. It raises hope that we can continue to risk reowning the parts of ourselves that the very language we speak demands we suppress, ignore, disown, and hide.

THE OTHER AND THE BINARY

Difference and exclusion are not incidental to language but are integral to how we create meaning. According to Derrida, this reliance on difference also leads to a tendency to see the world's complexity in terms of simplistic binaries: strong or weak, black or white, fish or fowl, gay or straight.

Western thought tends to cast any difference into opposing halves that between them exhaust all meaning. Binaries treat the world like a pizza on which you're only allowed to make one cut. Anything that doesn't fit one half or the other gets lost, squeezed out. But with gender, it's exactly this space in between—familiar binaries like masculine/feminine, man/woman, top/bottom, butch/femme, and real/artificial—that we want to explore, reclaim, and uphold.

At first these binaries look like two halves of a whole. A binary may be like a pizza on which you can only make one cut. but it is definitely *not* down the middle. If you look closer, most binaries look suspiciously like covert extensions of the series "good/bad," in which one term is always the defining one while the other is derivative.

For example, Man is understood as the universal term: what Man can achieve, one small step for Man, the his-story of Mankind. Woman is cast as Other—blank, mysterious, exotic, unknowable— ready to be inscribed with whatever meanings are left over. In fact, femininity, motherhood, and sexuality are often thought to con- taminate the idea of Man-hood. For Woman, biology may not be destiny, but it is almost all of meaning.

If He is strong, forthright, and independent, then She must be weak, mysterious, submissive, and dependent. If He is defined by his pursuit of sex and procreation, then She must be defined as the object of desire, the vehicle for procreation.

By being not-Man, She serves to give Him meaning. Yet apart from Him, She has almost no independent meaning herself. She is almost entirely derivative. As the queer gender, Woman ends up being not the "opposite" sex but the derivative one.

CENTERS

Trying to be inclusive won't help when it comes to binaries. For instance, take the ever-popular "spectrum of gender." It's an effort to be more inclusive when it comes to gender.

But it's inevitably anchored by the only two *real* genders—Man and Woman. All those "other genders" are either strung out between them, like laundry drying on the line, or circling around them in orbit like some kind of errant Sputnik.

Because it sets the terms of discussion, the first term of the binary acts as a center that is insulated from being questioned. Thus we endlessly debate the meaning of Woman but not Man, homosexuality but not heterosexuality, blackness but never whiteness, transgender but never *normal* genders.

Binaries are like the black holes of knowledge: Nothing ever gets out. And nothing new can get in. That's why a new nonbinary gender is as impossible to imagine as a new primary color.

In the end, binaries are not just a curious way we have of understanding the world. They are political. They are about power. They create hierarchies—male/female, white/black, colonial/native—that produce winners and losers.

FINAL TRUTHS

Derrida's attack on language and meaning is part of his larger assault on Western thought. For Derrida, the history of Western thought is a procession of grand truths. These monolithic truths are called transcendent, and at various times these have included the one God of the Catholic Church, the perfect reason of Immanuel Kant, and the infinite cycle of point-counterpoint-synthesis of Hegel and his dialectics. As each monolith succeeds the last, it is declared to be universally true—for all people, in all societies, and at all times.

Derrida is infuriated by the Western compulsion to create totalitarian forms of knowledge. He sees in this a kind of selfishness, a tyrannical desire to pronounce final truths and to judge other cultures' and other people's way of viewing things.

For gender, this means once again that anything that is small, unique, and personal, that might open up new ways of being or understanding ourselves in the world, is considered meaningless. Thus we are all called to kneel before the monolith of Sex. Sex is not a property, and "What sex are you?" is not a valid question. Rather, sex is a demand—sex yourself! Everyone must have a sex; it can never be lost or avoided, it cannot be nonbinary, and it must be recognized and tracked from birth.

AVOIDING THE VOID

For Derrida, the entire tradition of Western thought from Plato on down is dominated by an essentially dishonest quest for what is universal and certain. We seek these transcendent truths because we demand some sort of "superhard" knowledge that is always reliable, always true. We want it to rescue us from the void, from the unknown.

In the West, the void of not-knowing is not a fertile place, a place of stillness or potentiality. For us, it remains mostly an abyss— a place of irrationality where nothing is known for certain. In such a place there can only be darkness, chaos, and an endless descent into madness (and maybe weird new genders).

PURSUIT OF THE SINGULAR

Final, singular truths may make perfect sense when we're dealing with measurable physical phenomena, such as the heat of a star, the size of an atom, or the hardness of rock, but make almost no sense when it comes to highly politicized bodily characteristics such as sex, gender, desire, or race. We equate truth with unity. In fact, our attempts at truth are usually attempts to find and restore an underlying unity of things.

Perhaps this stems from our Judeo-Christian tradition, in which the one, true God of the Hebrews is good and virtuous, and the faithful slaughter their enemies who believe in many gods—who are therefore false, duplicitous, and evil. In any case, we discount difference as a noise in the system, a problem to be resolved, a veil hiding the real unity of things.

In philosophy, as with gender, multiplicity equals error, a failure to find that which is singular, real, and True. This creates an economy of repetition, in which similarity circulates endlessly but nothing new ever emerges. The True is what can be repeated. It eliminates messiness and complications. Which is a pretty good description of where we are with gender today.

ALTERITY

What is at stake here is how we deal with difference, with alternatives—what theorists call *alterity.*

Derrida's attacks on language, reason, and meaning were the result of a deep anger at Western ways of thinking that tended to suffocate alterity and difference. Advocates of this social order sought to amplify Western power and insulate it from attack by claiming it to be transcendent, by speaking in the voice of universal rationality.

Esoteric as this may sound, it was anything but a dry academic pursuit. Derrida, and other French postmodernists who followed, had lived through some of the worst moral crimes of the 20th century—from of the technical "rationality" of the Nazi death camps to the use of scientific progress to exterminate the entire civilian populations of Hiroshima and Nagasaki. These philosophers became deeply suspicious of what social progress on that infinite upward spiral really meant when it came to the human spirit.

This work also bred an intolerance for any sort of totalitarian beliefs that might ever again lead to such blind obedience and destruction.

The postmodernists came away from the killing fields of World War II determined to attack monolithic worldviews, and to introduce uncertainty, doubt, and intellectual spaciousness into the system.

Derrida called for decentering knowledge, which would enable alterity to breathe, that would enable the excluded and erased to reemerge. In this sense, postmodernism is a philosophy of the dispossessed, perfect for bodies and genders that are unspeakable, marginalized, or simply erased.

Derrida inaugurated a new practice, called *deconstruction,* to help accomplish this decentering. Deconstruction sought to demonstrate how any given set of truth claims was only possible because of a prior set of assumptions that didn't "show" once they were in place. Later we'll be deconstructing the assumptions that make homosexuality, intersexuality, and opposite sexes possible, as well as a distinction between "real" bodies and drag and transgender bodies. All of these truth claims are heavily dependent on unstated assumptions about sex, sexuality, what counts as real, physicality, and what is natural.

Deconstruction reveals that a given Truth is not transcendent, that it is dependent upon other small-t truths, and that it is *culturally constructed.* Deconstruction thus is as much political tool as philosophical method. It is about power. And it is an antidote to universal Truths.

REALNESS, CONSTRUCTEDNESS

Deconstruction has proven a sharp weapon in the wars of thought, as it was meant to be. Yet it has also caused confusion. Showing that something is culturally constructed has become synonymous with saying that it is artificial or untrue. However, saying that something is constructed is not the same as saying it is not real. For instance, feminists frequently complain that postmodern debate over the constructedness of gender ignores the real suffering of women.

It is precisely this suffering that makes it so important for us to explore the constructedness of gender and its political effects on women. Derrida's constructedness is not opposed to real. Rather, it is an attack on the very idea of Real.

Derrida means to demolish the fantasy that through reason we can reach a privileged place outside of language and culture where we can stand above the world and pronounce with utter certainty what is True. He wants us to forgo our arrogant dreams of infinite upward spirals and deal with the real-world effects of selfish demands for certainty on those who are smaller, weaker, and different.

Derrida's constructedness is like what you get when you use a cookie cutter on a freshly rolled sheet of dough. There is no truth to the cookies, and no particular shape was any more inherent in the dough than any other. And when you eat one, there's no doubt that the other cookies are "real" too.

A NEW SUBVERSION

Obviously, Derrida's work is deeply subversive to our traditional ways of thinking and our notions of truth. It is not so much a set of truth claims itself as a set of tools for dismantling other forms of knowledge and truth claims. It was inevitable that gay, feminist, and gender theorists would appropriate the postmodern tool set. Predictably, this appropriation has had unpredictable results.

Of all the things we know about ourselves, first and most fundamental are things about our bodies: things like sex, sexuality, and gender. And of all forms of knowledge we have, among the most oppressive—those that present themselves as the most transcendent—are things like sex, patriarchy, and heterosexism.

As a set of tools, postmodernism is remarkably free of political content. It is the perfect two-edged sword: It cuts everything equally on both sides. Once these theorists began deconstructing nasty, oppressive institutions like heterosexism and patriarchy—something they very much wanted to do—they found themselves drawn to deconstruct sexual orientation, gender, and sex—something they were not at all sure they wanted to do. And because the binary categories of male/female, boy/girl, gay/straight are among the primary ways we come to know ourselves, theorists soon found themselves in the tricky business of deconstructing the Self as well.

5. HOMOSEXUALITY: FOUCAULT AND THE POLITICS OF SELF

"Sexuality as a term did not appear until the beginning of the 19th century. What had been some 300 years earlier just so many disparate urges, inclinations, and activities were delineated as a problematic set of traits and drives that supposedly define a central aspect of human nature...[and]...define us as sexual subjects."

C. G. Prado, *Starting With Foucault: An Introduction to Genealogy*

SELF-KNOWLEDGE

If Derrida had deconstructed thought, it fell to another French philosopher, Michel Foucault, to deconstruct the thinker. Like so much of postmodernism, Foucault was addressing something "upstream" in Western thought, which is filled with notions of finding *our self*, knowing *our self*, and being true to *our self*.

How this particular sense of the self and its place in the world—this subjectivity—originated is a question we seldom consider.

We assume the Self is transcendent—it just exists, constant and universal. And we reason from there.

It was exactly this certainty that Foucault wanted to attack. Just as Derrida considered how we think about the world as constructed, Foucault understood how we think of the Self as constructed, no less a cultural artifact than a vase, a chair, or a building.

As he put it, "The individual…is not the vis-à-vis of power; it is, I believe, one of it prime effects."[1] In other words, we think of the individual as a conduit for power, something it acts on and through. But power is also what first creates us as specific kinds of individuals.

For instance, when I was growing up, I simply thought of myself as a *boy*, a strange and geeky one and often very unhappy, but a boy just the same. People had always suspected that I was queer, and in fact I tried for several years to live as a gay man. I blush to admit that I made a great gay man. And except for the fact that I had a female lover and wasn't sexually attracted to men, I might still be one today.

Over time, I realized I was a transsexual, as the literature put it: a woman trapped in a man's body. Which helped explain why it always felt so crowded inside.

I learned to think of myself as a woman. Although, after all the hostility I encountered, increasingly I felt—often painfully—that I was somehow an imitation woman. Since I was still involved with my lover, I also learned I was really a lesbian transsexual. A few years later, as the discourse shifted, I became transgender.

All of these subjectivities felt quite real at the time. Yet on another level, none of them really made any sense; they all felt less like something integral to *me* than reflections of what others think is important about me.

How did I come to know myself as *these* particular selves? Why were these the available choices? Whose interests did they serve? And how did knowing myself in these ways move me to willingly alter, shape, and even manage my own behavior?

These are exactly the kinds of questions Foucault wanted to ask. We all want to *be our selves*. But what, Foucault asked, does it cost to know your Self?

Although he was gay, Foucault refused to identify as homosexual. He saw that kind of identification as a form of self-knowledge to which he didn't subscribe. So perhaps it is only logical that he launched his most passionate attacks on the politics of Self through that notorious 19th-century invention, the Homosexual, and on the very idea of sexuality itself.

THE SEXUAL CONFESSION

"We demand that sex speak the truth...we demand that it tell us our truth."

"Since Christianity, Western civilization has not stopped saying, 'To know who you are, know what your sexuality is about.'"

Michel Foucault, *The History of Sexuality: An Introduction*

According to Foucault, Western cultures have an elaborate knowledge of sex that goes back for centuries. But until the Enlightenment, this sexual knowledge was primarily concerned with technique and pleasure. Sex held no special secret or meaning. There was nothing to be learned from it except perhaps how to enjoy it more.

Certainly, there was an awareness of sex and transgression. Things like public nudity, masturbation, lewdness, debauchery, and congress with minors were all understood to be offenses to good civil order and public morality. They were punished accordingly by the courts.

But following the Enlightenment, all this began to change. The Catholic Church was increasingly influenced by the monastic practices of monks and other ascetics, for whom the self-denial of celibacy was the paramount expression of spiritual devotion. The Church's approach to sex began to shift in important ways, which would eventually move sex from the periphery of minor transgressions and place it as the central issue of morality.

For a monk, almost any passing yearning might grow quickly into a serious threat to vows of celibacy, poverty, and humility. Purity of thought was as important as purity of body and acts. Following this reasoning, the Church began to focus on the importance not only of sinful acts—things one had done and should repent—but sinful desires—things one only wanted or thought about.

Impure thoughts—random daydreams, and sudden urges—became dangerous new sources of mortal sin, even when they were never acted upon. The Church urged people to confess everything about their sexuality in ever more exacting detail. The more humiliating and private and difficult to tell, the better.

This new concern for sexuality demanded of people new forms of vigilance. It became something one searched out in oneself, something that required rigorous nonstop self-examination. No longer something to be enjoyed, if with discretion and restraint, sex had become something that threatened salvation.

Sexuality was transformed into something akin to truth. To know one's Self increasingly meant to know one's sexuality. Knowledge of sex had become increasingly disconnected from pleasure. It was focused almost solely on how to prevent sin.

Sexuality had emerged, not as a pleasurable appetite that occasionally called forth unruly behavior, but as *the* central problem of living a moral life. And the Church—prompted by obscure rituals created by monks to scourge themselves of impure thought—emerged as its sole arbiter.

THE PERVERSE IMPLANTATION

This new form of self-knowledge—Sexuality—enabled the Church to exert enormous new power over people's lives and to invade every corner of their most private thoughts. Moreover, it enabled the Church to get people to willingly manage and maintain their own behavior, even when they were alone and far from the papal gaze.

We are now so accustomed to thinking of sex as a central moral issue that it's hard to appreciate just how far we've drifted from awareness of sex as just another pleasure. Sexual knowledge was once simply a means to better and more pleasure.

But consider that other, more basic appetite: hunger. The politicization of food is almost nonexistent. We fulfill our appetite for food a dozen times a day. Yet no one bases their primary social identity— vegan, meat-eater, lacto-vegetarian, French fry addict—on it. No one considers our appetites to be a source of self-knowledge. And we are not moved to discuss or confess what and how we eat. Eating has almost no consequences for morality or sin, and we don't struggle to come to terms with our hunger the way we do our sexuality.

Today we want to know almost everything about our sexuality, *except* perhaps how to enjoy it. We almost never mention technique and proficiency to one another.

We have become confessing animals. We confess our sexual secrets not only to priests but on talk shows, in books, and to therapists. And we confess not only what we have done but also what we like to do. We are like a group of leering teens, asking one another, wide-eyed, with barely suppressed giggles, "So what do you like to do?"

One of my dearest friends, who lights up whenever he puts on four-inch heels and a miniskirt, is absolutely certain that his cross-dressing is not just an innocent pleasure but a sign of deeper, darker character deformities that should be treated by a psychiatrist.

We even have a National Coming Out Day so that we can tell each other about our homosexuality. Sexuality and gender have emerged as central foundations for social identity.

DEVIANCE AND THE BIRTH OF NORMALCY

The growth of perversions is…the real product of the encroachment of a type of power on bodies and their pleasures.
Michel Foucault, *The History of Sexuality: An Introduction*

Had the issue of sex and sexuality remained confined to our rites of private examination and public confession, sexuality might have remained simply a problem of sin. But by the 18th century, with the rise of scientific approaches to human behavior, nation-states became newly aware of population shifts as a national concern. State bureaucrats began tracking everything from contraceptive use, illegitimacies, and birth rates to adulteries, family size, and marriage rates.

The emphasis on sexuality shifted once again. Sexuality became something to be managed for the public good.

Improper desire was no longer just a threat to decency or even a source of mortal sin. It was something that threatened society as a whole, that wasted an important national resource, and that, left unchecked, might spread.

From the belief that perversion was a pleasure that was unusual or unseemly, a new science of deviance and normalcy emerged. Along with it came a scientific rationale for the social cultivation of sexuality that was desirable and *natural*. Sexuality that was abnormal and therefore unnatural had to be stamped out. Starting in the late 1800s, doctors like Richard Krafft-Ebing and Havelock Ellis began obsessively cataloging every minor sexual deviation and thereby "brandishing the whole emphatic vocabulary of abomination," in Foucault's words. Masturbating children, female sexual hysterics, the insane, the mentally retarded, gerontophiles, pedophiles, zoophiles, and necrophiles all came under new scientific scrutiny.

Pleasure and desire were called to account for themselves, to step forth and offer an explanation. Sexuality was no longer just the great secret but something that held great meaning, which Science and Reason could unlock.

A SCIENCE OF SEXUALITY

Throughout Foucault's deconstruction of sexuality runs an immense skepticism toward the application of Science to pleasure and desire. He is especially angry about the construction of sexuality—this new form of self-knowledge that burdened each of us with a sense of our Selves as harboring an inner drive that must be watched, explained, and understood.

In Foucault's view, the institutionalization of sexuality led individuals to willingly manage their own private behavior in ways they would never have undertaken otherwise. This acquiescence allowed huge institutions—the church, the state, and medicine—to have new and invasive powers over people. Often those who suffered the most under this new Science—the different and the marginalized—were those with the most to lose. Sadists, masochists, transsexuals, cross-dressers, the intersexed, sissy boys, and tomboy girls—all were deemed *deviants* in need of *treatment*.

Until only 30 years ago, this list also included millions of homosexuals.

Today, noncomplaining children as young as three are still diagnosed with "Gender Identity Disorder" (GID) simply because they are gentle boys or tomboys, and sent for psychiatric treatment and behavioral modification. As doctors like Toronto's Kenneth Zucker explain, treatment is often intended to prevent them from growing up to be homosexuals as adults.

Behavior modification for girls may include punishment for aggressive or athletic behavior, and praise for looking feminine, and submissive behavior, including flirting with adult males. Rewards can include playtime, television, or dessert. For boys, modification may include punishment for playing with dolls or crying, and rewards for aggressive, dominant, or athletic behavior.

Strangely enough, this is something which feminists, gay rights advocates, civil rights lawyers, parental groups, transgender activists, and medical doctors still ignore. The American Psychiatric Association still sanctions such treatment, and you can reasonably hope for insurance reimbursement for subjecting your child to this sort of medical "treatment."

There is little doubt that such marginalized individuals have always been with us. Yet the Science of Sexuality is not concerned with seeing what is there. Instead, it is motivated by what Foucault called "a stubborn will to nonknowledge" which seeks "not to state the truth but prevent its very emergence."

But the new Science was not interested in knowledge *about* Sex, but rather power *over* it. It generated an entire taxonomy of latencies, perversions, deviance, and disorders. And it sought to impose on bodies and their pleasures a universal rationality, one that profoundly altered our relationship to our own desires.

From the 19th century on, sex would shift registers, moving from the realm of law, morality, and religion to medicine, normality, and disorder. And the centerpiece of this shift was the Homosexual.

ENTER THE HOMOSEXUAL

As the cause of gay rights advances, it may be difficult to recall the fear, anxiety, and disgust that attached itself to homosexuality for more than a century. In his autobiographical book *Cures,* noted gay historian Martin Duberman recounts enduring an invasive and demeaning succession of therapies in the late 1950s and early 1960s to cure his homosexuality.

Duberman was a sophisticated New York intellectual. If this experience was such anguish for him, what must it have been like for people who were less well-informed and well-connected. Indeed, it was not unusual for homosexuals to be subjected to electroconvulsive therapy—shock treatment.

If homosexuality was not spoken of in polite company, parents were still constantly vigilant for any symptoms of "latent desires" in their children, and many even worried about the slightest sign of "homosexual tendencies" in themselves. The purveyors of popular culture made sure homosexual characters died, preferably violently, at the end of films and novels. The detection and prevention of homosexuality was a national obsession, along the lines of a public health crusade. There was a kind of controlled hysteria about homosexuality, as if it were a silent contagion.

Yet homosexual acts were certainly nothing new. In fact they were familiar and well-recorded by the ancient Greeks, from whom we acquired so much of our aesthetics and philosophy. A Greek man (Athenian women were a different matter) might fully indulge himself with virgins, prostitutes, married women, boys, or sheep. Nothing he did sexually qualified him as a particular sort of person or established his social identity.

While homosexual acts were well-known, homosexuals were not. This was not because the ancient Greeks did not create problems about sex. They did, but their worries about sex were in a completely different register.

For the Greeks, the problem of sex was its proper use, not its direction. If a man indulged his sexual appetites to excess or became so consumed with lust that he was unable to function effectively, then he had a problem with sex.

By the 18th century, homosexual acts were understood (as they are today in 17 states) under the vague legal catchall of "sodomy," which designates acts that offend public decency. People who committed such acts were to be punished and shamed, but sodomy law was concerned with what people did, not what they were.

But in the mid 1800s, medical science began exerting its control over sexuality. Where "the sodomite had been a temporary aberration; the homosexual was now a species."[2] People who engaged in nonprocreative sex came to be seen as something dangerous, possibly even contagious carriers of a disease that needed to be isolated, diagnosed, and treated.

Where homosexual acts had been what one sometimes did, the homosexual person was something permanent, what one *was*. For the first time it was possible, even necessary, to identify *as* a homosexual.

Physically, the homosexual was overfeminized, delicate, and pretty, though sometimes he was big, muscular, and overly handsome. He might have a small penis, or in other cases an unusually large one. Psychologically, the homosexual was sensitive and fussy, yet also cunning and inventive. His behavior was brazen and predatory, yet also shy and demurring.

Like all medical pathology, homosexuality had a definite cause. For instance, lesbianism was caused by "fear of the opposite sex, fear of submission, fear of penetration, fear of rejection, fear of the unfamiliar (as contrasted with the familiar), fear of inadequacy, fear of rivalry...plus seduction by an older member of the same sex, seduction by another adolescent of the other sex, excessive masturbation, rampant narcissism, frigidity, and nymphomania."[3]

Now, 150 years later, we see the rise of a homosexual rights movement that articulates and understands its identity in almost exactly the same terms invented by 19th-century medical doctors to diagnose and prevent it. It is impossible not to cheer the success of this movement in establishing new rights for gay people in the workplace, marriage, and adoption. At the same time, it's impossible not to question the elevation of private sexuality as the basis for social identity. Is it at all strange to think of oneself *as a Homosexual?*

Of course it is important to be able to be honest with others about who we really are. But is there no more edifying or dignified basis for explaining that "are-ness" than with whom we like to sleep, or even whom we love?

Of course we should all have equal rights. But what about the right to be defined by something other than our sexuality or gender?

THE POLITICS OF SUBJECTIVITY

"The formation of a subject requires that it seem to each power-shaped subject that she or he is that subject naturally. If there is reflection on one's subjectivity, on what sort of subject one is, the aim must be to discover something about one's given nature, not to understand how one was produced as a subject. When it occurs, reflective introspection must be engaged in by an individual with a view to getting past the effects of enculturation to the 'real' self."

C. G. Prado, *Starting with Foucault: An Introduction to Genealogy*

Like Derrida, Foucault directs us again to the ways that language and meaning create what is True, and how Knowledge and Science are actually highly politicized. But he does so with an important difference: Foucault applies deconstruction to the Self, to our basic sense of who and what we are.

For instance, when discussing Foucault, I've been approached by more than one confused gay person with this sort of complaint: "It was one of the most powerful moments in my life when I finally came to terms with my lesbianism and came out to my parents. Am I now supposed to give that up?" Foucault's point is not to force us all out of our identities, as if that were any less oppressive than forcing us into them.

What he *is* saying is that it is not enough simply to recognize one's self as gay, however empowering that might be.

He wants us to go a step further and ask what it means to understand one's Self through a form of knowledge that scarcely existed 200 years ago, but which today forms the core of one's identity. He wants us to ask how such identities are created, what effects they have on us, and whose ends they serve.

Foucault wants to undermine our naïve belief in the Self as transcendent. He is showing how even this subjective sense of Self has a history and a pedigree, has arrived in response to specific cultural needs and demands. He wants us to understand that subjectivity can be a form of politics by other means.

The fact that so many different pleasures remain "on the books" as diseases suggests that, while gay rights advocates may achieve equality for some, the politics of homosexuality continues to leave many behind. The mechanisms for producing deviants remains as insidious as ever.

6. FOUCAULT AND THE DISCIPLINARY SOCIETY

"The central issue...is not to determine whether one says yes or no to sex...but to account for the fact that it is spoken about, to discover who does the speaking, the positions and viewpoints from which they speak, the institutions which prompt people to speak about it and which store and distribute the things that are said. What is at issue [is] the way in which sex is 'put into discourse.'"
    Michel Foucault, *The History of Sexuality: An Introduction*

DISCURSIVE POWER

The new form of power Foucault is talking about is called *discourse*, and it is central to understanding postmodernism, and more importantly, gender. In everyday speech discourse simply means a dialogue, a discussion between two people.

But Foucault means something closer to a social dialogue, a discussion society has with itself: a set of meaning-making practices.

Discourse is a set of rules for producing knowledge that determines what kinds of intelligible statements can be circulated within a given economy of thought. For example, in the discourse on gender, you can only say meaningful things about two kinds of bodies that will make sense. References to third genders will always sound fanciful, nonsensical, or just ridiculous.

Discourse is the "cookie cutter" we encountered in the chapter about Derrida. The social truths we have about gender have to do not with the body, but with the cutter.

THE PRODUCTION OF TRANSGRESSION

Two great discourses have attached themselves to the "problem" of gender transgression: medical/psychiatric and academic/feminist.

There will soon be a third discourse. Adherence to gender stereotypes has been such a deep social convention that courts and legislatures have seldom had to deal with it. As a result, the legal discourse on gender is still in its infancy.

A case in point: A GenderPAC intern recently suggested we track every state's legal definition of sex. I thought this was a great suggestion. To our surprise, we learned that only one state, Texas, had ruled what constitutes legal sex, and that decision was only a few months old. (In the year since discovering this, three more states have ruled on legal sex, leaving two in favor of recognizing sex changes, and two against recognition.)

But transgender people—whether they are cross-dressing truck drivers, gay employees who refuse to "butch it up," women who wear suits, or transitioning transsexuals—are becoming more visible and outspoken, and they are witnessing a dramatic expansion of the legal discourse on gender stereotypes.

The discourses have targeted four populations whose transgression of gender norms qualifies as pathological: cross-dressers, genderqueer children, transsexuals, and the intersexed. Both discourses use specialized practices to endow their pronouncements with authority. These pronouncements usually include:

* Specialized Vocabulary: gender dysphoria, prehomosexual behavior, fetishistic transvestitism, surgically altered males, ambiguous genitalia.

* Professional procedures: prognoses, physical examinations, field research, psychiatric diagnoses, case studies.
* Methods of documentation: scholarly articles, clinical charts, research studies, psychotherapy notes.

These discourses do not *study* gender transgression; rather, they create it by presenting these people as suspect populations. As controversial and problematic, such populations must be studied, explained, and understood, and perhaps their behavior must even be prevented.

This might be expected of medicine and psychiatry, which have long and unpleasant traditions of dealing with difference by branding it as pathology.

But it has been especially discouraging to see such strategies from feminist academics, who understand what it's like to be erased and silenced, to be made into some sort of strange, exotic problem. They ought to know better.

The emphasis is not on showing how the gender system delegitimates and silences difference but on revealing what transgender people *really* are *underneath*. Inevitably, the gender binary remains intact.

Female transsexuals are really men; cross-dressers are enacting a fetish that imitates women; "sissy boys" are confused or underdeveloped; butch girls have penis envy; butch women are identifying with the oppressor; and intersex infants aren't really intersexed but are actually girls and boys underneath. Through it all, transsexuals, drag kings, sissy boys, tomboy girls, cross-dressers, and intersexuals do not speak for themselves but are spoken for and about; they are objects *of* discourse, not participants *in* it.

There is an emphasis on realness, imitation, and the ownership of meaning (male mannerisms, women's clothes) that recenters and restores the Truth of binary gender. Although this is articulated in the voice of medicine and academia, of Science and Logic, there is nothing reasonable or objective about it.

At issue here is not the well-worn graduate-school debate over whether the "soft" sciences can be as objective as the "hard." Rather, knowledge of gendered bodies cannot be objective in any meaningful way because the pursuit of it requires a whole host of assumptions about what counts as real, the binary nature of gender, the boundaries of normal, and so on.

Objectivity is meaningless when it comes to gender and queerness because the very notion of queerness, the production of some genders *as* queer, and the search for their origin and meaning are *already* exertions of power.

Part of the confusion here, as Derrida notes, is our use of the verb *to be* to initiate something into language. We use *to be* for objectively verifiable facts, such as, "It is 95 degrees today."

But we also use it when we are making strong assertions, such as "Boys are masculine," or "There are only two genders," and for things that are merely propositions, such as "This space is safer if it's for women only."

This causes confusion because these statements all use the same form of is-ness even though they are very different types of statements.

A MICRO-POLITICS OF POWER

In progressive politics we think of power as something held by the state and exercised from the top down upon the individual. It is solid, concrete, and visible: You can see its operation by watching the police, the army, or the courts.

This is repressive power: the power to silence, wound, and punish. We fear this repressive power and the potential of the state to abuse the individual.

But discursive power operates in a different register entirely. Where gender is concerned, the main exercise of power is not through repression but *production*. Discursive power produces specific kinds of individuals, with specific bodies, pleasures, and sexes.

For instance, it much easier to get men to be manly if they

understand that the meaning of their very bodies and identity in the world *is* masculinity. Even the word *manly* is inseparable from the identity Man.

In the same way, it is easier to get women to be feminine if they understand themselves to be feminine beings in the physical reality of their breasts and hips, in periods and pregnancy, in size and musculature and psychology. Again, even the concept of womanly is inseparable from Woman. What could seem more ridiculous—at odds with reality itself—than the masculine woman?

This kind of discursive power does not operate from "the top down" but from "the bottom up." It is not central, but diffuse and capillary. It is not held by authorities and institutions; rather, it is held by no one but exercised by practically everyone.

This is not the traditional power of the policeman with his nightstick. As philosopher Nancy Fraser notes, while the narrative of individual rights "still packs its liberatory punch...[t]alk of rights and the inviolability of the person is of no use when the enemy is not the despot but the psychiatric social worker" consulting a diagnostic table or a teacher disciplining a 5-year-old because "big boys don't cry."[4] We have centuries of experience and political theory to deal with repressive power, but we have practically none to deal with productive power. It is not even a form of power we recognize, which makes it difficult to think about.

Because of this, we may need new forms of politics to challenge discursive power. This is not only a civil power—like the rights to marry, vote, or equal employment opportunity. You can't just pass laws against this kind of power.

An attack on discourse involves an attack on the categories themselves. Most struggles for rights are sought in the name of one group or another. While the group may or may not win the power and legitimacy they seek, the categories of discourse are implicitly accepted by those on both sides of the fight.

For instance, blacks, women, gays, and transgender Americans all want their rights *as* blacks, women, gays, and transgender people. But what if part of the coming struggle for gender rights includes not only our rights *as* men and women but also the right *not* to be *only* men or women? What if it includes an end to the relentless production of a sex-binary society? This might include an end to mandatory sex assignment at birth and mandatory sex tracking on required legal documents like drivers' licenses and passports, alternatives to separate sex-binary public facilities, and an end to psychiatric discrimination against people seeking nonbinary sexes and genders.

The coming gender rights struggle will have to address not only civil rights, but something like social rights as well, including the right to be different, to different forms of subjectivity, and the right to experience ourselves outside of the usual binary categories.

This right is already being extended by an unexpected agent: the U.S. Census. People increasingly view themselves beyond familiar, narrow racial categories; e.g., Tiger Woods joking identification as "Cablanasian"—Caucasian, African-American, Asian. In 2000, the U.S. Census allowed citizens to self-identify their racial category. If only the rest of society were so accommodating.

This is close to the foundation of human rights: freedom of expression and our right to say and think and believe as we wish. How strange that this fundamental right is protected in so many venues, except one area so crucial to authentic social functioning—gender.

A BIGGER STICK

If discourse is a power that not only restrains but produces us as certain kinds of social actors, is it enough to explain the range of effects we see in the gender system—effects that stretch across nearly the entire plane of our contact with society? These effects also reach into our most private moments of contemplation of our selves and our bodies. The question is important because discourse alone hardly seems sufficient to explain the nearly universal constancy of gender.

Let's assume that all of us are born more or less complete human beings, able at birth to experience the full range of gendered emotions, identities, and expressions.

Even if we try to conform to one role or another, we should "leak" like sieves. How could anyone suppress half of themselves, minute by minute, even in their most private feelings? Conformity should be literally impossible.

Yet within a few years, almost all boys become masculine individuals who are deeply shamed—even in private—by any vestiges of their femininity. And all the girls will be feminine, avoiding any semblance of their masculinity. For example, a recent study showed that at ages 11 to 12, almost 96% of girls took part in sports. Within six years, by ages 17 to 18, the number drops to under 5%. And that trend holds roughly true across racial and economic groups.

It's possible to describe all this as "Nature's way," the inevitable effect of hormones and chromosomes. But this hardly seems a sufficient explanation. To explain a power this pervasive and robust, operating in private just as effectively as in public and producing subjects so uniform in how they look, act, and dress, Foucault needs to give us something bigger—a better account of power, a bigger stick. He finds it, strangely enough, in the history of prisons.

VISIBILITY AND THE INTERNALIZED NORM

"A gaze which each individual under its weight will end by internalizing to the point that he is his own supervisor, each individual thus exercising this surveillance over, and against, himself."

Michel Foucault, *The Passion of Michel Foucault*

According to Foucault, the central problem of lawbreaking had originally been punishment, whether being privately tortured in the king's dungeons or being publicly flogged in the town square. Although brutal, these punishment techniques were not very effective at deterring lawbreakers. First, fear wears off and is sharpest only when police are nearby. Second, while capital punishment might work in small towns, where everyone knew the person punished and people tended to stay put, by the 1800s the world of rural towns-people was giving way to big, anonymous, mobile populations of urban centers. Third, with the spread of democracy, lawbreaking was increasingly understood as an offense against society that required not only punishment but installing social norms.

So the prison was invented. The prison was not only a humane alternative to torture and flogging, it embodied a set of new techniques for managing populations that would instill internalized norms of behavior.

The central method the prison used was continuous individual surveillance combined with rigid schedules and endless drill. Each inmate was housed in an open, private cell—a small theatre perpetually visible from a central command post.

Every hour of the day was scheduled and observed. Inmates performed continuous ordered drills, known as *dressage* in the military. The slightest infraction was met with punishment and loss of privilege. Every waking moment was tightly programmed: a time to bed and to rise, so much time for washing up, rules for where prisoners could be at what times, rules for the arrangement of cells, daily inspection, and so on. The smallest misbehavior was monitored, normalized, and punished: tardiness, sloppiness, loudness, inattention and idleness, personal cleanliness, moving too quickly or too slowly.

The organizing principle of the prison system was no longer simply punishment or public display. The prison was designed to change inmates' consciousness of themselves. Its aim was to make them, under infinite observation and control, infinitely self-conscious and self-controlling.

Moreover, the prison sought to instill in these new citizens-to-be not only a sense that what they had done was deviant and abnormal, but that they themselves were deviant and abnormal, that they needed not just to obey the law but to change who and what they were. Over time, inmates would internalize the gaze of the jailer and learn to regulate their own behavior, watching for the slightest deviation.

Physical punishment of offensive social actions became a process of remolding the consciousness of offensive social actors. Control through the fear of punishment had been exchanged for the fear of being abnormal, and the latter was to prove the much stronger motivator. The prison would produce something new: not ex-offenders but normalized citizens, individuals ready to police themselves, down to the smallest detail, even when alone and out of sight.

THE DISCIPLINARY SOCIETY

"Culture is organized to regulate the individual's use of time (tardiness, slowness, the interruption of tasks) activity (punishing inattention, negligence, a lack of zeal; speech (punishing idle chatter, insolence, profanity; the body (punishing poor posture, dirtiness, lapses in stipulated reflexes); and finally, sexuality (punishing impurity, indecency, abnormal behavior)."
Michel Foucault, *The Passion of Michel Foucault*

Over time, the techniques embodied in the layout and rituals of the prison slowly made their way into general society—especially the military, where breaking down recruits' sense of individuality in boot camps and instilling in them a sense of self-consciousness and obedience is central to making them into soldiers.

But the techniques of the prison were also adapted in schools, factories, and offices—anywhere it was desirable for a small group of people to efficiently instill norms of conduct, accountability, and self-consciousness in a large group.

For instance, in schools each child is assigned a separate seat, arranged in an orderly, well-spaced grid in which each individual is visible to a central authority. Each moment is scheduled: a time for arrival, for homeroom, for study, to get to the next class, or to eat. Each area has its rules: what you can do in the classroom, the hall, or the cafeteria. With minor adjustments, the same could be said of the modern office.

Foucault's story dovetails nicely with Ian Hacking's contention in *The Taming of Chance* that about the same time the prison emerged—old ideals of an orderly, rational, God-given world began to give way to a world ruled by chance, probability, and statistics. Only a few decades earlier, the idea would have been completely foreign, even heretical: There was only God's way, perfect and complete.

But by the 1800s, the notion of a God-given world that was pre-determined and preordained was increasingly replaced with "new laws, expressed in terms of probability. They carried with them the connotations of *normalcy* and of *deviations from the norm*. The cardinal concept of the psychology of the Enlightenment was simply human nature. By the end of the 19th century, it was being replaced by something different: normal people."

What became increasingly important was not just performance but conformity. In such arrangements, anyone who behaved differently quickly stood out. Moreover, they also quickly became excruciatingly self-conscious of it. There is a Japanese saying that neatly captures this: The nail that sticks out will be hammered in.

Foucault used the term *discipline* to refer to this new arrangement of power. He declared that modern society had quietly implemented an "indefinite discipline," in which the techniques of the prison had become a central organizing principle for creating conforming people.

Disciplinary society aimed to produce "docile bodies"—perfect, uniform citizens who had internalized a sense of personal visibility, self-consciousness, and social norms. This process produced individuals for whom the greatest fear—even in their most private moments and particularly in their private sexual activities—was to be or be thought abnormal.

Society had learned to arrange itself in such a way that difference would not need to be punished but could actually be prevented—and not by authorities but by individuals themselves, not just intermittently when in public but continuously in private as well.

Foucault has produced a fair description of the mechanics of gender in modern daily life. We are subject in daily life to a continuous dressage of gender. In this continuous drill, each individual's every move is weighted with gendered meaning: vocal inflection, watch size, heel height, hair length and overall musculature. We habitually consider whether we stand with our feet together or apart, sit with our legs or ankles crossed, hold a glass with a pinkie up or down. We monitor our choice of cigarettes, whether our shirts and belts fasten from left to right or right to left, what colors we choose what sports we play, whether we prefer to eat a thick piece of red beef or lightly steamed veggies. We observe whether we tend to ask questions or make statements, inspect our nails with the fingers bent or extended, point with our wrists broken or firm.

We do this in public, where—conscious of others watching us and own continuous visibility—we join them in watching and judging ourselves. And we do it in private, policing and regulating our own behavior just as avidly as if we were on display.

Gender conformity is made possible through a sense of permanent visibility, a strong consciousness of shame before others, a rock-solid belief in what our bodies mean and that meaning's utter transparency, and the continuous dance of gender that attaches binary meaning to every facet of our waking lives.

LIMITS OF DISCOURSE

Sex is the central problem for all the things we want to say about gender. Gender, conformity, and norms may be products of cultural practice, and they may even be produced through the power of discourse. But where does that leave us with Sex?

Sex appears to come from a place (in Butler's memorable phrase) "on the far side of language," beyond the effects of culture. As the ultimate universal Given, Sex reminds us that—no matter what we say about gender—there is still a fixed, biological basis for all this in the flesh.

But what if Sex is already a gendered way of looking at bodies? What if Sex is already gender, so that the distinction between the two is no distinction at all? What if Sex—the original Given, transcendent and universal—could be deconstructed?

[70]

7. ALL TOGETHER NOW: INTERSEX INFANTS AND IGM

"There is nothing abstract about the power that sciences and theories have to act materially and actually upon our bodies and our minds, even if the discourse that produces it is abstract. It is one of the forms of domination, its very expression."

Monique Wittig, *The Straight Mind*

BODIES AT THE MARGINS

As Foucault once pointed out, the effects of discursive power are hard to see once a discourse is in place. Once we *see* gay, black, female, or transgender people, it's hard to imagine that they weren't always there. We imagine the cultural discourse about them just popped up in response; rather, it was the discourse that created such identities in the first place.

To clearly see discursive power at work, we need bodies at society's margins. Margins are margins because that's where the discourse begins to fray, where whatever paradigm we're in starts to lose its explanatory power and all those inconvenient exceptions begin to cause problems.

We can see the marginalization of such bodies as evidence of

their unimportance. Or we can see their marginalization as important evidence of the model's imperfection and begin to admit how the operations of language, knowledge, and truth have shaped our consciousness.

Once we might have turned to women, gays, transgender people, or even racial minorities for this kind of understanding. But as each of these groups has won greater or lesser degrees of social legitimacy, it has become necessary to look a little further out to find a really marginal, inconvenient body. We need a body that is still off the grid of cultural intelligibility, one that hasn't "set" yet into a socially recognized identity. What we need, of course, is a *herm.*

Cheryl Chase is a "true hermaphrodite." This is a very rare thing, since most intersex people are "only" pseudo-hermaphrodites.

When most people hear the word *hermaphrodite,* they're apt to think of a person born with "both sets of genitals," although this is actually impossible. *Hermaphrodite* is actually an archaic medical term, and the correct term is *intersex.*

According to Brown University medical researcher Dr. Anne Fausto-Sterling, one in every 2,000 births is intersex. As intersex activists say, these are children born with unexpected genitals, which is to say their genitals are perhaps worse, maybe better, or at least every bit as good as yours and mine (well, *yours* anyway).

Cheryl founded the Intersex Society of North America (ISNA), a national intersex advocacy group, and cofounded (with me) Hermaphrodites With Attitude—an intersex protest group, in itself a pretty rare thing. I just call her the Head Herm.

Along with www.ISNA.org, another great information source on intersexuality and related issues is www.BodiesLikeOurs.org

CONSTRUCTING CHERYL

"Cheryl" was born as "Charlie," a fairly happy, well-adjusted little boy. His doctor, however, was not as happy or well-adjusted.

For one thing, it must be admitted that Charlie had a pretty small penis. For another, Charlie had "ovaries" that contained both testicular and ovarian tissue.

Language is again a crucial issue here, especially at the margins, where labeling is the first discursive act that determines how a thing is seen and understood. For instance, if a boy has an ovary, is it still an ovary, especially if it also contains significant amounts of testicular tissue, as Cheryl's did? Medicine gives us no nonbinary options here, although the term *gonad* would do nicely enough.

Charlie was a year and a half old when—after tests, consultations, and diagnostic conferences—doctors decided that Charlie was actually a Cheryl. This meant his small penis was actually an abnormally large clitoris. So they cut it off.

Following the treatment protocols for a diagnosis of intersexuality, all evidence of Charlie's existence was hidden. Boy's clothes and toys were thrown out and replaced with girl's clothes and toys. Out blue, in pink.

Cheryl/Charlie's parents were warned to lie to her if he ever asked about her history, because the truth   intersexuality and surgery— would permanently traumatize the child. Doctors feared that acknowledging a history of intersexuality would undermine the sense of gender identity they had created in the child through secrecy and surgery.

Charlie had become Cheryl, but at an enormous price. The operation had removed a lot what the doctors thought was Charlie, but it also removed most of his erotic sensation, and along with it baby Cheryl's future ability to have an orgasm.

THE ABC'S OF IGM

"Intersexuality is a psychiatric emergency on the part of the doctors and parents, who treat it by cutting into the body of the infant, even though the adults—as the ones in distress— are the real patients."

Cheryl Chase

"The Academy is deeply concerned about the *emotional, cognitive, and body image* development of intersexuals, and believes that successful early genital surgery minimizes these issues."

Press Release on IGM from the American Academy of
Pediatricians (emphasis added)

"Knowledge is not made for understanding; it is made for cutting."

Michel Foucault, *Language, Counter-Memory*

The surgical procedure Cheryl underwent is sometimes referred to as intersex genital mutilation. IGM refers to cosmetic genital cutting that is performed solely to make intersex infants resemble normal males and females. The definition of IGM does not include the small fraction of surgeries that are preformed to cure functional abnormalities, urinary obstructions, recurring infection, and so on.

It was not until the 1950s that IGM became a common pediatric practice. Prior to that, unless infants were born with genital deformities that caused ongoing pain or endangered their health, they were left alone. Today, according to Fausto-Sterling, about 1,000 infants are surgically altered for cosmetic reasons each year in U.S. hospitals, or about five every day.

Advocacy organizations like ISNA and GenderPAC do not advocate raising intersex children without a sex, which is a social impossibility anyway, at least right now. They do advocate forgoing permanent genital alteration of infants for strictly cosmetic reasons until they have grown old enough to participate in life-altering decisions about their own bodies and sexual health, and to offer informed consent.

LANGUAGE AS THE REAL

A pediatric nurse in one of my presentations complained, "But you don't mention all these tests we run to find out the infant's real sex." The discourse on intersex infants is concerned with discovering what binary sex they "really" are, so we can "fix" them properly. The possibility that intersex infants' sex might not be immediately available to us, that they might not have the sort of binary sex the doctors are so anxious to locate and assign, just doesn't register. Neither does the possibility that intersex bodies have nothing to tell us, or that these infants are whatever sex they are because that non-binary outcome appears to the medical community (and indeed to most of society) as a logical impossibility.

As Cheryl notes, intersex is the sex that doesn't exist. First because it's always another sex "underneath" and, second, because as soon as it appears, we erase it. Whatever sex we "discover" in intersex infants' bodies is highly dependent upon what markers we choose— hormones, genitals, overall body structure, chromosomes, and gonads—and how we prioritize them.

For instance, a *Primetime Live* segment included a bizarre exchange in which Dr. John Gearhart, a pediatric genital surgeon from Johns Hopkins University Hospital, showed Diane Sawyer (and her viewers) slides of intersex infants' genitals, while she tried to guess each infant's real sex.

That surreal interchange went something like this:

Diane: That's a male, right?
Doctor: Nope. A female. This one?
Diane: A female.
Doctor: No, a male.
Diane: Now this is certainly male. That looks like
   a small penis.
Doctor: Sorry, another female. This one?
Diane: Female?
Doctor: Male. This?
Diane: Male?
Doctor: Female.
Diane: Shee-it!

Words are real; bodies are not.

There is no pretext of transparency here: We don't fit the words to the bodies; instead, it is the bodies that must fit the words. The only language we have for herm-bodies is directed toward pathologizing—and thereby delegitimating—them.

Nor can we raise the usual argument—"It's Nature's way"—when Sex is questioned. Clearly, Nature has other things in mind, even if we don't.

In this vein, I once tried to help a network producer who was searching for an intersex person to interview. He was interested only in one who had been surgically misassigned the "wrong sex." Our conversation went like this:

Producer: We're looking for someone whose sex was misassigned and who was then raised as the wrong sex, like John/Joan.

Me: How do we know if it was the wrong sex?

Producer: If they were really male but assigned female, or really female but assigned male.

Me: Okay. But what if they were really intersex?

Producer: Right. I get your point. But we're looking for someone who was misassigned.

Me: But if they're really intersex, then any assignment would be a misassignment.

Producer: Right. I get your point. Really.

Me: Why don't you interview Cheryl Chase? She/he's well known and very articulate.

Producer: Cheryl was misassigned?

Me: Yes. She/he was raised as a boy, then they decided she/he was a girl.

Producer: So she's really male?

Me: No, she/he's really Cheryl.

Producer: Right. I get it. I really do. But she's really a girl, right?

Me: Well, to me she/he looks like a woman, but do you mean hair, hormones, chromosomes, or genitals?

Producer: You know. Her *real* sex.

Me: Cheryl's real sex is intersex.

Producer: Uh-huh. I get it, honest. But can you give me an inter-sex person who was misassigned?

DISCOURSE: A PRACTICE WITH EFFECTS

Cheryl/Charlie had no say in what was done to him/her, nor had she/he complained that anything was wrong with him/her. The doctors and nurses involved were not spiteful or intolerant. On the contrary, they were dedicated healers, trained in pediatrics and deeply committed to Cheryl/Charlie's well-being. IGM is always considered compassionate surgery. Everything was done for his/her "own good."

Cheryl's mutilation did not result from the top-down power held by big institutions. Unlike that reliable villain, the State, the power involved was not that of repression and negation, so common when sex is involved. In fact, the discourse of Sex where Cheryl was involved did not *restrain* her Sex, but rather interpreted it, compelled it, and *demanded* it.

Her transformation from Charlie to Cheryl was carried out in a micro-politics of power: small, impersonal judgments and practices that involved myriad individuals, power that was held by no one in particular but exercised by practically everyone—except, of course, Charlie.

The power involved was productive, using language and mean-ing to interpret her genitals as defective, to produce her body as intersexed, and to require that she be understood through a lens of normal male and normal female. Through a series of silences and erasures, it socially produced a new person, one with a new name, history, wardrobe, bedroom decor, and toys.

This is not the familiar "big stick" approach to power that requires policemen, courts, and legislatures. That is something we are familiar with; at least it is something we know how to fight. The power that attached itself to Charlie's body is a different kind of power entirely, one we have little experience in dealing with, let alone have strategies to counter.

The Science involved in Charlie's surgery was also of a different order than we are accustomed to. That Science is logical, objective, and impartial. But the Science that has attached itself to herm-bodies is not disinterested at all, but rather interested in the most urgent way with preserving the universality of Sex and with defending society's interest in reproduction. In fact, one of IGM's basic rules is that any infant who might one day be able to become pregnant as an adult must be made into a female.

This kind of Science is characterized by a deliberate nonknowing, by its refusal to recognize the most obvious facts of the infant bodies before it. It is remarkable for its sturdy denial of any facts or interpretations that might contradict its own intentions.

THE SCIENCE OF SEX: PARTIAL, PASSIONATE, POLITICAL

Medical theories of Sex, like so much of theory, are concerned with the resolution and management of difference. Intersex infants represent one of society's most anxious fears—the multiplicity of Sex, the pinging under the binary hood, a noise in the engine of reproduction that must be located and silenced.

This kind of Science is not limited to bodies. Its psychiatric counterpart is called Gender Identity Disorder, or GID. GID does for insubordinate genders what IGM does for insubordinate genitals.

In GID, noncomplaining children as young as 3 and as old as 18 are made to undergo treatment that includes behavioral modification, confinement to psychiatric wards, and psychotropic medication, all because they transcend binary gender norms and/or cross-gender identify. These treatment measures are intended to help the child fit back into a defined gender role.

In many cases the psychiatrists who treat GID believe that norm-transcending "sissy boys" and "tomboy girls" are more likely to grow up to be gay, and GID treatment is designed to prevent homosexuality in adults. Yet gay activists largely ignore GID because they represent gay and lesbian Americans, and a 3-year-old doesn't have that kind of identity yet.

Of course the effort to regulate gender in children is not limited to those "at the margins." We have a host of social practices designed to masculinize boys and feminize girls that start at birth. For instance, infants who cry are more likely to be described as angry by adults who think they are boys, sad if they think they are girls. Caregivers are more likely to stroke and caress babies if they think they are girls and to bounce them if they think they are boys.

Up until a few years ago, the U.S. government was funding research into the best treatments for norm-transcending kids. Tax dollars were appropriated to pay for a new sort of knowledge manipulation: the prevention of "sissy boys." This has helped fuel a new counterscience devoted to providing biological basis for homosexuality. Our power *over* such bodies is enabled by the kinds of knowledge we create *about* them.

By asserting that the knowledge and language we create is transparent and objective, we confer enormous authority to it. We insulate it from criticism and deny its political origins; we justify excesses that might otherwise be unthinkable. At the margins, Science no longer asks but tells. Nature no longer speaks the truth, but is spoken to. Here, where our narrative of Sex breaks down, Knowledge finally bares its teeth.

IS IDENTITY POLITICS PERMANENTLY TROUBLED?

Cheryl can be understood as a genitally mutilated female, a genitally mutilated male, a transgender individual, an intersex individual, a man who sleeps with women, a woman who sleeps with women, or even a man with a vagina. This proved to be a real obstacle when Cheryl dealt with identity-based groups.

When we approached the board of a national women's organization for help, the organization's representatives responded that IGM was a terrible practice, and someone should stop it. But why, they wanted to know, was IGM a women's issue?

We pointed out that the overwhelming majority of infants diagnosed as "intersex" are otherwise unremarkable children whose clitorises happen to be larger than two standard deviations from the mean—an arbitrary measure equal to about three eighths of an inch. It turns out birth sex is like a menu. If your organ is less than three eighths of an inch long, it's a clitoris and you're a baby girl. If it's longer than an inch, it's a penis and you're a baby boy.

It is a startling example of the power of language, knowledge, and science to create bodies to realize that, if pediatricians agreed to increase this rule to, say, three standard deviations from the mean, thousands of intersex infants would be instantly "cured."

On the other hand, if they decided to decrease it to one-and-a-half standard deviations, one third to half of the female readers of this book would suddenly find themselves intersexed, and therefore candidates for genital surgery.

But if it's in between, you're a baby herm: The organ is an enlarged clit, and it gets cut off. The pediatrician will apologetically explain to your parents that you were born genitally "deformed," but—through the miracle of modern Science—they can make you into a "normal little girl."

Of course, this never happens in reverse. No pediatrician will ever apologetically explain to your parents that, "I'm afraid your son's penis is going to be too big, maybe eight or nine inches long. No one will ever be attracted to him but homosexuals and oversexed women. If we operate quickly, we can save him."

To help board members of the women's organization to understand, I showed them how to make a diagnosis. Holding up a thumb and forefinger about a quarter inch apart, I said, "female." Moving them about three-eighths of an inch apart, I said "intersex." I repeated this finger movement from "female" to "intersexed" over and over until heads began to nod.

Since many intersex infants were "really" women, this made IGM a women's issue. The board members even accepted Cheryl—

a true hermaphrodite if ever there was one—as a woman.

> Unfortunately, several board members insisted that since they were a women's group, I had to articulate everything in terms of "intersex girls," a term with no meaning that contradicted everything I was trying to tell them.

Flushed with success, I asked a gathering of national gay organizations for their support on IGM, too. After what I thought was an impassioned presentation, they all agreed that IGM was a terrible practice and someone should stop it. But why, they wanted to know, was IGM a gay and lesbian issue? I pointed out that many intersex infants are heterosexualized as infants, surgically altered simply to ensure their bodies can accommodate a penis during intercourse.

Even worse, some doctors perform IGM out of the antique fear that girls with large clits (which no man likes) will repel potential husbands (which every woman needs), interfere with penetration (which every woman enjoys), and increase their chance of growing up to be masculinized lesbian women (which practically no woman wants to be). IGM was no longer an intersex issue or even a women's issue; it had become a gay issue.

I decided to cap my success by addressing a meeting of transgender organizations. Genderqueerness was their beat. This would be a walk in the park. And it was. They understood IGM right away. It was, they all agreed, a terrible practice, that someone should stop. But why, they wanted to know, was IGM a transgender issue?

Soft-pedaling Cheryl's identities as intersex, female, or lesbian, I focused like a laser on gender stereotypes. I pointed out that Cheryl had changed from one sex to another: She was transgender. Even more, IGM was a tell-tale example of enforcing exactly the kind of rigid, narrow, outdated gender stereotypes that hurt transgender people. In addition, a significant minority of transsexuals have some sort of organ development (such as hormonal imbalances and small or partial gonads) that could easily have gotten them diagnosed as intersex.

After extended discussion, IGM became a transgender issue.

Of course, none of these groups was ill intentioned or predisposed toward excluding intersex issues and IGM. They were all progressive, committed, and compassionate. Yet if national feminist groups even suspected that doctors performed clitoridectomies on thousands of baby girls each year, they would try to shut down hospitals across the country. If gay rights activists suspected that doctors were using hormones and surgery to erase thousands of potential lesbians each year, queer activists would be demonstrating in the halls of hospitals and lobbying in the halls of Congress.

But none of these scenarios have happened, all because an arbitrary definition means that these infants aren't female or possibly lesbian or even transgender. They're this other thing called intersex, which is not an issue for women or gays or transgender people; it's a medical issue. Presented with an enormously damaging and barbaric practice that harms thousands of kids, no group was able to embrace IGM as an issue. The rules of identity meant that intersex infants— the noise in the system—didn't fit.

It's enough to make you wonder if identity politics is permanently troubled. For that, we need Judith Butler and the critique she mounts of politics in the age of identity.

8. CAN SEX HAVE OPPOSITES?

"Does sex have a history? Does each sex have a different history, or histories?"

> Judith Butler, *Gender Trouble:*
> *Feminism and the Subversion of Identity*

Sex has no history. It is a natural fact…it lies outside of history and culture.

> David Halperin, "Is There a History of Sexuality?"
> in *The Lesbian and Gay Studies Reader*

"Somewhere in the 18th century, sex as we know it was invented."

> Thomas Laqueur, *Making Sex:*
> *Body and Gender from the Greeks to Freud*

INESCAPABLE KNOWLEDGE

It feels ominous that a number of people have warned me about including this chapter, anxious that any attempt to deconstruct Sex itself would be so far-fetched that it would undercut the book's credibility and alienate readers.

Attacking the transcendence of any immediate perceptual given, such as skin color or sex, always sounds a bit implausible at first.

For instance, skin color is so compelling that most people can't help but see race when they look at bodies. Like Sexes, bodies appear to actually be—in some fundament beyond culture, language, or discourse—of various races.

Yet recent Eastern European immigrants to the United States have had to learn that they were white. Because while skin color was just *there*, whiteness—at least as we view it in the United States—is a uniquely American concept. As is blackness, owing to our national history's uniquely pernicious "one-drop" rule, whereby a single drop of African-American blood was held to render a person nonwhite.

Even today, most Caucasian-Americans see only white and non-white. But many African-Americans see an entire spectrum, because in a racist system such distinctions are crucial in the access to privilege. One study in the 1940s noted that black teens had more than 150 terms for skin color, including half-white, yellow, light-brown, medium-brown, brown, chocolate, and blue-black, each with its own reality and meaning.[5]

Although race and skin color are *out there* somewhere, whites and African-Americans are not seeing the same thing. Color may be there, but everything they mean in terms of whiteness and blackness is clearly not.

Critical race theorists and others have increasingly drawn our attention to the ways that race can be deconstructed. So perhaps it's not too much to hope that we can deconstruct Sex as well—just a little. This is important because a central problem for gender theory has been that no matter what telling points are made about gender, Sex lurks right behind, pulling everything right back in the direction of immutable biology.

"When it comes to reproduction there are," a student reminded me at a college event, "inevitable differences between boys' and girls' bodies you can't get around." Of course there are. But the question has always been how much difference that difference makes.

Sex is not just about reproduction and the interesting property of some bodies to produce offspring when they are rubbed together at the right time. On the contrary, Sex is the primary property of all human bodies, including those that cannot now or never will participate in procreation, such as infants, adolescents, transsexuals, the very old, women past menopause, sterile and infertile people, vasectomized men, hysterectomized women, the seriously infirm, and some intersexuals.

If Sex is not just about reproduction, it is not just about genes, XY chromosomes, and hormones either. Sex is introduced to explain skeletal structure, mental aptitude, posture, emotional disposition, aesthetic preference, body fat, sexual orientation and responsiveness, athletic ability, social dominance, shape and weight, emotional lability, consumer habits, psychological disposition, and artistic ability. It is also supposed to explain any number of so-called "instincts," including the nesting instinct, the maternal instinct, and perhaps even the Budweiser instinct.

THE FAR SIDE OF LANGUAGE

In fact, sometimes it appears our culture has created a new sex industry devoted to producing Sex 24 hours a day, seven days a week—not by putting people to work on street corners in short skirts to solicit cash from passersby, but by putting them to work in white coats in well-lit laboratories to solicit grants from universities and foundations.

Hardly a month passes without some arm of the sex industry announcing the results of a new study confirming the differences between men and women. The results are then endlessly recycled by popular culture and consumed by us as a reassurance of the fundamental binary nomenclature of all bodies.

For instance, as I write these paragraphs, I notice that the Discovery Channel is rebroadcasting its hour-long special *The Science of the Sexes,* a program devoted to the neonate biology that produces *opposite* sexes. Of course, the program is silent on the definition of what counts as "difference," or "opposite," or the overwhelming evidence of neonate biological similarity. Because who would be interested in that?

The narrator recounts in suitably hushed tones an experiment showing how girls and boys react differently when a glass barrier separates them from a parent. Boys try to get through; girls cry for help.

But surely many boys and girls reacted similarly. I suspect some responded with a mixture of reactions. Some reacted in totally unique and unexpected ways. About this we hear nothing. Nor do we hear about boys like me (who probably would have sat down and wept) or girls like Leslie Feinberg or Martina Navratilova (who probably would have annihilated the barrier). Why? Because we don't count—we're problems, not data.

In fact, in the hundreds of shows about neonate sexual development I've viewed over my lifetime, I can't recall a single one that mentioned—even in passing—the fundamental similarities between male and female infants. Difference is what we want, and difference is what we get. Even studies that produce results that have only statistical significance—say, an experiment that finds a reliable sex-based difference in three out of every 10,000 infants—are held dear, although their effects are so small as to have no practical value.

Indeed, as Anne Fausto-Sterling has noted, research that fails to find evidence of male/female differences is thrown out; it is unpublishable. Researchers cannot even apply for a grant to study such similarities because there is no interest in them. We spend millions of dollars creating and documenting sexual difference while any sixth grader with a pen and a few reams of paper could cite endless evidence of sexual similarity.

The very term "opposite sexes" itself gives us a sense of the overheated cultural impulse that drives the sex industry. This social institution has reversed the order of knowledge, so that Sex is no longer something about bodies; rather, bodies have become something about Sex.

As Butler notes, unlike gender, "'physical features' appear to be in some sense there on the far side of language, unmarked by a social system" {p. 114}. They are implacable, indisputable, and absolute.

Deconstructing Sex is impossible. It is a center for which there truly appears to be no Other. The body becomes a text that is always and only read one way. Any questioning of Sex is suspect. It must explain itself quietly, set its terms narrowly, and offer its arguments tentatively. Sex itself requires no explanation. It is the perfect transcendent Given—original, primordial, and indisputable.

THE FIRST GIVEN

"Language casts sheaves of reality upon the social body, stamping it and violently shaping it."

Monique Wittig, *The Straight Mind and Other Essays*

But if Sex is such an obvious and natural fact of bodies, why is it something that children must be taught? Why does it take so much trial and error for sexed knowledge to take hold, for the small discoveries of playing doctor to take on the overwhelming and pervasive meanings we carry into adulthood?

What if, like skin color or gender, Sex is both there *and* constructed? How is such a construction be accomplished?

Constructions can still be compelling. I am reminded of the first time my friend Tony pulled down his jeans to show off his new $33,000 penis. As I looked on with fascination, he began razzing me with various invitations, all of which had the words "my dick" and "suck" in them.

I quickly found myself immersed in the usual complex reaction I have to the idea of giving head, until it dawned on me that   given the donor site for his graft—I would be sucking off his forearm.

We can get a glimpse of this in the work of Emily Martin. Martin went looking for the medical and scientific facts of sex and reproduction, and she found gender instead to be the sort of upset-the-apple-cart stuff that would never, ever be used by the Discovery Channel.

Start with gametes, the foundation for reproduction. The sperm is inevitably characterized in a narrative of virility, aggression, and mobility. Eggs are…well, your basic egg is usually described as a combination of Sleeping Beauty and a sitting duck. Plump, round, and receptive, it waits—passive and helpless—for the sperm to throw itself upon her moist, quivering membranes. Conception itself is equally memorable. The sperm push furiously at inert egg until one of them finally penetrates deep into the warm, defenseless tissue.

It is not that the facts are wrong—quite the opposite. Rather, it is that the meaning we give them creates a cross between a Harlequin bodice-ripper and a *Dirty Harry* film. The role of the .357 Magnum ("the most powerful handgun in the world") is played by that veteran character actor, Mr. Penis, and a sperm is Clint Eastwood with rabies, just looking for an egg to "make my day."

Necessarily so, since the simple facts are pretty barren. A gamete does this, and a chromosome does that. Like the body itself, the facts of sexual reproduction have resonance only if we imbue them within a meaningful narrative, a context. In this case it's the cultural narrative of power and gender, as we understand it in a sexist, heterocentric culture.

Medical texts render gamete production in a similar manner. The testicles' production of two trillion little flagellant critters during the male's lifetime is described in metaphors of activity, creation, and the miracle of biology.

Egg production, on the other hand, is a big disappointment, miracle-wise. Females have all the eggs they'll ever need at birth. As they age, the eggs age too, pulled off the shelf (yawn) at a rate of one per month, and the longer they're on the shelf, the more they deteriorate. If the testes are Marines on Paris Island, the ovaries are all inventory problems and K-Mart.

Even conception does not escape this treatment. Menstruation is described by means of a narrative of loss, debris, and failure, because it entails wasting half of one potential person-type cell that might have grown up to be you or me (well, you anyway), along with several teaspoons of lukewarm fluid.

Ejaculation also involves the loss of several teaspoons of lukewarm fluid, along with enough potential person-type cells to repopulate this planet and several others. However, ejaculation is unfailingly described as a life-giving phenomenon: potent, energetic, and hearty. The notion of waste is nowhere to be found.

As with body temperature or race, the facts are there, but the meaning is added. This is knowledge of a different order, made not for understanding but for politics, for reading a narrative of difference, of masculine and feminine, onto reproduction.

If reproduction is constructed, then could the sexed body be constructed as well? Could our understanding of Sex itself be in some way a result of our use of meaning, image, and metaphor?

To answer that question, we need Thomas Laqueur.

DISAPPEARING BODIES

"The notion of sex made it possible to group together, in an artificial unity, anatomical elements, biological functions, conducts, sensations, and pleasures...a causal principle, an omnipresent meaning, a secret to be discovered everywhere: sex was thus able to function as a unique signifier and as a universal signified."

Michel Foucault, *The History of Sexuality: An Introduction*

Laqueur's work is an attempt to give Sex a history, to reveal its hidden assumptions, and to show that our understanding of Sex has a human origin. Laqueur begins with the female orgasm, which had historically been considered necessary for conception to occur. Naturally early medical texts gave a lot of space to facts about female orgasm. But by the 19th century, female orgasm disappeared. Within decades, doctors were hotly debating whether such a thing even existed.

For the anxious reader, let me quickly reassure that the female orgasm was rediscovered in the late 1960s. Unfortunately, by then it had acquired unexpected baggage in the form of a G Spot and the truly sexually impertinent female ejaculation.

Female ejaculation had always been around, but it was written off as urine or other secretions. Men ejaculated; the more demur sex did not. Science's and popular culture's rediscovery of the female ejaculation was not a result of more and better knowledge, but rather a shift in attitudes that allowed us to view the female body in a new light.

The more Laqueur hunted for the "lost" female orgasm, the more the reassuring specter of a fixed—and binary—Sex retreated. In its place he found a body thoroughly politicized and culturally obedient, a body whose contours, functions, and meanings shifted dramatically through history.

Facts were produced and dismissed, emphases shifted, categorizations changed, organs were redrawn, and names were changed to protect the innocent. In short, Laqueur began to find a history for opposite Sexes.

ONE BODY, ONE SEX

According to Laqueur, since the first Greek anatomists—about two millennia ago—there had been one body and one Sex and it was Male. The Female body was considered to be essentially similar in nature, but an inferior version lacking in some vital essence that caused it to be smaller, more delicate, and come with an *inny* instead of an *outty*.

This was not because Greek and later European doctors were stupid. Nor was it because they didn't see what was right in front of their eyes when they opened up a body. Rather, wherever Science looked at bodies—male or female—it saw similarity, because that was what it was looking for. The reigning paradigm of Science until the last few centuries had been one of finding similarity.

For instance, Natural History stressed the overall appearance of things, their relationship in the order of things, and their completeness as wholes. Cats and dogs might be lumped together because of their similar appearance, shared cultural status in art and literature, and common niche as household pets.

As for male and female bodies, there was plenty of difference to go around, but difference was understood through social roles and the conventions of culture. Male and female difference was located in how that body behaved, where it fitted into the order of things, and its cultural role, not in any deep-seated, organic difference in bodies themselves.

The understanding of male and female bodies as basically similar reflected the larger belief in a world that was singular and divine and natural. The task of Science was to find and document the essential relatedness of things.

But over the last 300 to 400 years, a new paradigm arose and, with it, new ways of seeing.

The world was understood less as God's than Man's, and Science's task was not to find the divine underlying similarity in a thing's design, but rather to catalog and classify the differences among things in ways that might help Man to understand, use, and control them.

This Enlightenment Science stressed difference over similarity, ordered pieces over wholes, separation and distinction over connectedness, isolation over context, and the breakdown of inner structure like the skeleton over the totality of outward appearance. With the emergence in biology of Linnaeus's chart of species, Science's task had clearly become dividing all living things into separate, distinct species and classifying them accordingly.

THE SEAT OF DIFFERENCE

"But a penis and vagina are fundamentally different. There's no way you can get around that."

A reader's comment on an early draft of this chapter

"Instead of being divided by their reproductive anatomies, the sexes [were] linked by a common one."

Thomas Laqueur, *Making Sex:*
Body and Gender from the Greeks to Freud

But what of the seat of sexual difference for us: the penis and vagina? Aren't they manifest evidence of opposition and difference?

Doesn't the entire argument Laqueur is making founder upon them?

In fact, for most of recorded history, the vagina did not even have a separate name. And since it clings to the viscera with no particular shape of its own, it was drawn pretty much in the same shape as the penis, but pointing in instead of out. The penis and the vagina were considered merely two varieties of a common organ: one fitting over or into the other.

This may sound odd to us, but it is not the least bit far-fetched. The penis and vagina and their surrounding tissues evolve from exactly the same underlying fetal tissue, share the same physical location, and have a common underlying structure (penis-clitoris, labia-scrotum, etc.). They also share a common function in reproduction, and they even behave in similar ways: stroking each produces arousal, secretion, and orgasm.

In fact, starting from a paradigm of similarity, it's perfectly reasonable to see the penis and vagina as providing, not primal difference, but strong evidence of bodies' underlying and inherent similarity.

OPPOSITE SEXES

Sometime in the 18th century, sex as we know it was invented. As Carol Travis has noted, it is no accident that theories of difference flourish precisely when the differences in question begin to fade. As social roles began to grow together and less distinct, "difference that had been expressed with reference to [social conventions of] gender now came to be expressed with reference to sex" and a "language of similarity began to be replaced by a language of incommensurable difference."

As a dominant and monolithic Center, Male was not differentiated from Female so much as Female—the Other—was differentiated from Male. Female was used as a blank surface where whole new truths could be written. The notion of differentness extended itself over the Female body like a shroud.

The ovaries, which—like the testes—had historically been known simply as the gonads, were given separate names and meanings. The vagina was named, to make it more distinct from the penis.

Menstrual blood was separated from all other fluids and discharges—particularly from all other kinds of blood and bleeding—and given an enormous weight of cultural meaning. Along with the ovary, menstrual blood became the very definition of Femaleness, and the immediate, visible symbol of femininity.

In the late 1600s, the first Female skeleton was assembled for study using the most feminized cadaver that could be found—especially wide hips, narrow rib cage, small head, and tiny hands, wrists, ankles, and feet.

This choice was made not because there were new bones to be shown, but rather to display and anchor difference. From then on, anatomists would draw the Female skeleton so as to maximize its divergence from the Male. The two sexes, in other words, were invented as a new foundation for gender.

ARE OPPOSITE SEXES NECESSARY?

It is easy to believe that in this story of opposite Sexes—if we decide to give it any attribution at all—is simply an example of modern Science doing its stuff. The scientists were ignorant; we know better—end of story.

Yet the rise of two-sexed bodies did not result from our knowing more. So what dictated the rise of the two-sex model? As we saw with the rise of a new Science of Homosexuality, everything that was necessary to derive one model or the other had been common knowledge for centuries.

More and better Science did not dictate the rise of a two-sexed body for the simple reason that "the nature of sexual difference is not susceptible to empirical testing. It is logically independent of biological facts. Two incommensurable sexes were, and are, as much the product of culture as was, and is, the one-sex model." Each model is just that: a model for organizing and contextualizing the body that "is logically independent of biological facts because already embedded in the language of science, at least when applied to any culturally resonant construal of Sex, is the language of gender."[6]

More facts and better Science can never resolve such debates because all they can offer is more ammunition to each side. In the final analysis, what bodies, organs, and fluids mean, and whether the glass of similarity is half full or the glass of difference half-empty, are not problems of Science, but of politics.

Laqueur also asks the obvious questions: Why sex? Why this particular collection of parts and why this particular assembly? Why do we need Sex to be present for us on all bodies at all times, even those not engaged in reproduction, even those (like mine) forever unavailable for reproduction?

In spite of all the knowledge we already have, it remains permanently unclear what we expect Sex to tell us, and why we need to have a Sex for every body (lest it appear to us utterly, piteously, frighteningly naked).

IS VISUAL LANGUAGE TRANSPARENT?

Even if we reject Laqueur's attempt to provide us with this story of opposite Sexes, in a way it doesn't matter if he's literally correct or not. What is important is that Laqueur's historical survey provides the basis for an alternative way that bodies could be understood, for organizing the surface of the body in other than two oppositionally different Sexes.

In doing so, we see that while Sex is not necessarily inevitable and essential, it might have a human history after all—not Sex as the capacity to reproduce, but Sex as this infinite quality pervading every aspect of our bodies and separating humanity into two distinct binary halves.

Laqueur forces us to confront the frightening, dislocating idea that—like our textual language—the visual language of bodies isn't transparent either. In other words, body parts aren't necessarily or only what we see them to be, because, as belief changes, vision can change too. We learn to see things a certain way, and by seeing them that way, we rely on our belief in that vision to inform us about what is ultimately *real* and *out there*.

This might seem another prescription for the irrationality and uncertainty of the Abyss, where nothing is known or definite. Yet a little dislocation and even apparent irrationality are the price we pay for a certain kind of freedom, in which other ways of knowing can emerge and survive.

Perhaps Foucault came closer to the truth in his essay "Nietzsche, Genealogy, and History" when he observed that "Nothing in man—not even his body—is sufficiently stable to serve as a basis for self-recognition, or for the understanding of other men."

9. POSTMODERNISM AND ITS DISCONTENTS

Postmodernism has generated a powerful set of tools for dismantling arguments, revealing their hidden assumptions, and diminishing their power so that difference can emerge. That's great for the struggle for gender rights, because that's exactly what we want to do. Not only because the gender system remains an oppressive "this box for girls" and "this box for boys" mode of thought, but because it's completely inert.

While the last 30 years have seen new rights granted to women, gays, and transgender people, this new access and privilege has still left issues of primary gender—of masculinity and femininity—remarkably untouched. Gender stereotypes appear as pervasive, "natural," and inevitable as ever.

It may be that binary gender is so fundamental to social reality that it may be impossible to evolve the discourse. We may need to nuke the discourse—to completely undermine it. This is something that postmodernism, with its focus on subverting universalist claims of knowledge and meaning, is well-equipped to do. At the same time, postmodernism has come under fire for its own perceived limitations. We know postmodernism's strengths, but what are its weaknesses?

AN ARGUMENT ABOUT ARGUMENTS

I recently spent two very lively hours with a college student group critiquing and deconstructing ideas about sex, sexual orientation, gender expression, and gender identity. Toward the end of the discussion, one exasperated young woman who had been watching in silence finally raised her hand to ask, "But what's your point? What are you trying to prove?"

Her frustration is common among those who encounter postmodernism for the first time. We are accustomed to each theory putting forth its own claims about what is real and true.

As Foucault observed, we are condemned to produce truth in order to live in society. We must produce truth as surely as we must produce wealth. Postmodernism's own truth claims are about the *nature* of truth claims. By working "one level up," so to speak, it pretends that it escapes promoting universal Truths and normative assumptions—the very problem it attacks. Of course it does not escape this at all.

It sometimes appears circular and without a point, since it is not making its own claims about what really is but rather providing tools for dismantling other people's claims about what really is. For example, by politicizing Thought, Derrida denies us the luxury of thinking objectively about bodies. He forces us to think about the language, logic, and meanings we apply to bodies.

By politicizing Knowledge, Foucault makes us consider how the kinds of things we want to know *about* bodies—their pleasures, dress, and reproductive capacity—gives us power *over* them. He denies us the luxury of innocent truths, forcing us to acknowledge that our truths are imbedded in our politics.

Thus the frustration many people experience when confronting postmodernism may begin with the obliqueness of thinking "one level up." But frustration is also a consequence of the difficulty of having to think about thought, of questioning the meaning of meaning, of losing the innocent use of reason, truth, and language. The frustration is not a sign of failure; it's the point of the exercise.

THE LIMITS OF CRITIQUE

Whether the field of inquiry is anthropology or women's studies, literary criticism or queer theory, postmodern scholars eagerly critique and complicate discourses that are oppressive. They have created an immense and growing literature of critique, deconstructing everything from the heterosexism to whiteness, from colonialism to the Western literary canon.

The bias toward critique is part of Derrida's foundation for postmodernism. Derrida places the same faith in Critique that traditional philosophers like Kant had in Reason. Critique is understood as progress because it enables new things, or at least different things, to emerge. Critique is therefore itself political action for the better.

Sometimes this works. The energetic critique of the gender system has helped provide new legitimacy for those on its margins—including transsexuals, intersex people, and cross-dressers.

Meanwhile, critiquing the mainstreaming of homosexuality has helped us reenergize the value of queerness, especially where fairies, butch/femmes, transpeople, and drag are concerned. Yet the emphasis on critique has meant that postmodern approaches to politics often seem to stress subversion as an end in itself.

Feminist theorists in particular have been quick to point out with irritation that deconstructing and subverting the identity of Woman will not provide equal pay for equal work or build shelters for battered women. This is obviously true, and these are obviously important causes. But, just as arguing that providing better health care for women won't overthrow centuries of patriarchy, it's also beside the point.

No one expects better health care to overthrow the patriarchy. They expect it to improve women's health. Just as few feminists expected Kate Millett's landmark critique of patriarchy in *Sexual Politics* to protect a woman's right to choose.

In the same vein, the postmodern critique of Woman is not intended to open battered women's shelters. Rather, it is intended to help subvert the stereotypes of masculine men and feminine women.

Just as Millett once complained about the patriarchy, the cultural production of masculine men and feminine women is so universal that it's hard to imagine any alternative by which it might be contrasted and thus critiqued. This very universality—again as Millett correctly observed about male ascendancy—means that to move forward, we must first attack patriarchal thought's air of inevitability, the fiction that it is Nature's way.

This is a task for which postmodernism is particularly well suited. Moreover, it is not unreasonable to believe that male masculinity and female femininity remain remarkably intact 30 years into the modern feminist revolution in part because traditional feminism has been as loath as the ambient culture to embrace male femininity and female masculinity. So, to enable something new to emerge, a radical critique of gender may be just what the doctor ordered.

WHAT COMMUNITIES (AND NORMS) ARE GOOD FOR

Along with postmodernism's emphasis on creating room for difference is a distrust of norms as being anything but oppressive—a reimposition of the Same under the guise of the Good. Because social groups cannot exist without shared norms of structure and meaning, postmodernism sometimes appears reflexively suspicious of community, often equating it with tyranny. The same can be said of its approach to institutions and bureaucracies—those things that sometimes seem composed of little more than norms, standards, and procedures.

Thus, it is unable to propose any notion of group action that is positive and rewarding. Such freedom as postmodernism envisions is the purely negative freedom found in isolation and separation, in strictly private acts and meanings.

It is similarly unable to imagine any interaction with the institutions of culture—with courts or civil rights groups—that might lead to any kind of freedom rather than a reimposition of old oppressions. In this we realize that postmodernism is still lacking any vision of constructive social engagement and political action. Indeed, it is innately suspicious of mobilizing communities for political action. For activists whose task is organizing for political change, this is a serious shortcoming. Finally, as scholar Martha Nussbaum has pointed out, postmodernism's antagonism toward norms means postmodernism cannot tell us why subverting gender norms is any more or less good than subverting, say, norms of human decency.

Actually, this is a bit of an overstatement. Postmodernism is not antagonistic toward norms per se, but toward transcendent norms that masquerade as universal.

It seems to presume an audience of conscience, of good readers who recognize (without being told) that imposing norms of sexuality and gender is bad but imposing norms of decency and free speech is good. This is, it must be said, an entirely modernist presumption.

THE PREDICAMENT OF TRUTH

"If truth does not exist, if merit is merely an expression of power, if there is no objective reality, then meaningful discourse is impossible and the hope of a just and equal society is a hoax."

Alex Kozinski, *The New York Times Book Review,*
November 2, 1998

A frequent complaint of Foucault's critics is that he seems to dance just out of reach, demolishing each attempt at Truth while coyly refusing to offer his own. Where, they ask, is *his* version of what is true? What does *he* propose as the alternative? This, of course, is exactly what he cannot provide.

Foucault understands statements of universal truth to be a form of politics—an intellectual fascism, a way of taking the universal voice in order to seize power while at the same time immunizing itself from criticism. Following Foucault often appears to be a one-way ticket: deconstructing practically everything while constructing almost nothing.

As one sympathetic critic observed, postmodernists fear being labeled naïve—or even worse bourgeois—more than they fear being wrong. They are afraid to speak lest their own hidden assumptions stand revealed.

Yet if Foucault is unable to offer us capital-T truths, if he is unable to speak to us with the voice of objectivity, is he then unable to offer us truth at all? This is an important question for activists, whose work demands that they conceptualize and communicate how the world is and how they think it should be.

Without an objective view of the world, without an idea of what is true, how can we be sure if we are thinking and acting rightly? For that matter, why should we think or act at all?

The ongoing culture wars in academia over multicultural curricula are another facet of this problem with objective truth and values.

On one side are those who assert that raising up the traditional Western canon hides the worst sort of intellectual colonialism, one that only values the work of DWM's (dead white males).

On the other side are those for whom multiculturalism represents a creeping relativism, one that would destroy meaningful standards of artistic or literary merit in the name of political correctness, placing the output of every culture or group on equal footing.

Yet giving up on the universal voice, on transcendent Truth, is not the same as giving up on truth entirely. As one of the 20th century's greatest philosopher's, Isaiah Berlin, once remarked, the answer is not relativism but pluralism—making room for others.

We might well declare that there are only two genders, or a 100, or even none, because gender is entirely constructed. But we need to qualify our assertions with the understanding that these are not just statements of reality but political statements as well; they serve certain agendas, they empower or erase certain bodies. This is the case even when we act with the best of intentions, and especially if we think we have the only such Truth.

AN ABSENCE OF AGENCY

Postmodernist theorists clearly want us to understand that discourse is a force to be reckoned with, producing everything from binary thought and docile bodies to language's transparency and the homosexual. But this argument doesn't come without a price. To begin with, if discourse is so all-powerful, then freedom is impossible. We can no more escape discursive power than we can our own subjectivity.

If our subjectivity—our internal sense of our Selves—is so determined by discourse, how can we ever get outside it? If we are doomed always to understand ourselves as female or homosexuals or transgender people, then what is the use of struggle? How can we ever know if we're thinking what we think, or only thinking what we're supposed to think as women, or gays, or transgender people?

Although postmodernists clearly intend for us to fight back, if discourse is so all powerful, it's hard to explain why we should bother. In fact, it's hard enough to explain how theorists such as Derrida or Foucault were able to escape the clutches of discourse and send back their analyses. How could we ever do likewise?

Discourse becomes like the Borg on *Star Trek:* "Resistance is futile." In making us the cookies to discourse's cookie-cutter, postmodernism seems to rob us of agency—any ability to act on our own.

In *Gender Trouble,* Butler tries to turns this argument inside out by embracing the contradiction: It is only by assuming these various identities that we achieve agency and become intelligible social actors. In her view, construction is not something opposed to agency but is the necessary ingredient for agency.

While this is a smart approach, I wonder whether it doesn't still leave many questions of agency unanswered.

Yet in the latter half of the 20th century, homosexuals, "girls," the genitally confused, and Negroes not only achieved new civil rights, they emerged as new things—gay, women, transgender people, and African-American (or black)—that homophobic, sexist, transgender-phobic, and racist discourses had never envisioned.

In other words, these groups changed the discourse. The problem is that postmodernism is unable to provide a coherent account of how this came about.

> Postmodernists can point out that the power of discourse is still overly determining. While such individuals may have changed the discourse, they still have been unable to alter the requirement that they *be* gay or female or transgender or black.
>
> Girls must still grow up to be women, and women must still be feminine. Gay people must still come out as homosexual. Transsexuals must still be understood in terms of "real" men and women.
>
> Apparently, we can have more equality as individuals, but we cannot *be* different kinds of individuals. We can have rights, but only by first agreeing to occupy the identities society demands of us.

THE PERSON BEHIND THE SUBJECTIVITY

Another problem for postmodernism is the way it grapples with subjectivity—with our intrapsychic experience of ourselves as individuals. One of its signal achievements is politicizing subjectivity. We now see how culture and discourse shape who we are and how we understand ourselves, and we no longer take either for granted.

At the same time, the conviction that culture produces us as individuals means that postmodernist theorists are loath to follow theory into individual consciousness. This is the messy realm of how we actually feel and what we can do about it: practically the only thing of interest if you're a living, breathing person.

This leaves theorists in the paradoxical position of having to explain by means of discourse how our thoughts and feelings are produced though discourse even though they lack any real desire to engage with how we think and feel because—as they argue—all that stuff is already over-determined by discourse.

This is a problem very like the issue of agency. Yet deconstructing subjectivity is not enough. Theory at some point will need to engage with us as individuals. It is not enough to deconstruct someone's *docile body* or the *dressage of gender* they live in without engaging how that *feels* for him or her.

For instance, I was recently trying to buy a blouse at the Gap. It reminded me of an old television commercial set at a tennis tournament, where as soon as someone mentions "E.F. Hutton," the entire stadium goes silent and everyone—players, fans, ball boys—stops to listen.

This little shopping outing was like that. Every time I'd try on a blouse, it was like most everyone in the store—customers and sales staff—would stop what they were doing to watch this man trying on women's blouses.

It was intimidating. It was scary. No one exactly harassed me, but I can't say I felt exactly safe either. After a few minutes, I was sweating, my heart was pumping, and I felt very, very ridiculous.

Why, I wondered silently as I left the story, *do I feel scared and ridiculous?* I know better. Helping people to overcome this kind of bumpkin behavior is what I do for a living. Why are ridicule and the implied threat of unpleasant social (or even possibly physical) consequences of disapproval so often the weapons of choice when it comes to gender? Why do they work so well, and what can we do to arm ourselves against them?

These are questions that postmodern theorists are still unable and unwilling to answer. They are not easy questions. But they are necessary questions if we are to go beyond deconstruction to the construction of something like a movement for gender rights.

OUT OF THE TOWER, INTO THE STREETS

This book grew out of a conversation with Angela Brown, one of my Alyson editors. We were discussing *GenderQueer,* and she observed that she'd studied "all that" theory in college, but it had since faded. I replied that hardly a day of gender activism goes by without my having to reflect on, or put to use, some bit of queer or gender theory. Yet I'm sure that Angela's experience is more common than mine is.

Feminist theory gave us feminism, and gay theory helped give us gay rights. But unless we bring gender theory out of the ivory towers and put it to work in the streets, we may be witnessing the birth of a major philosophic movement that succeeds in politicizing practically everything but produces practically nothing in the way of organized, systemic social change. And that would be a pity.

10. RACE-CRITICAL THOUGHT AND POSTMODERNISM'S "SECOND WAVE"

"We must redefine 'blackness'…we must redefine and restructure the central social categories…by which we conceive and understand our own social reality. What is required is a radical break from the narrow, race-based politics of the past.
Manning Marable, "Beyond Racial Identity Politics: Toward a Liberation Theory for Multicultural Democracy," in *Critical Race Theory: An Introduction*

"Maybe the target nowadays is not to discover what we are, but to refuse what we are."
Michel Foucault, *Beyond Structuralism and Hermeneutics*

THE UNIVERSAL VOICE OF CRITIQUE CRITIQUING THE UNIVERSAL VOICE

One last major criticism of postmodernism needs to be made. By now, it should be clear that the critique of the universal voice is intended to highlight silences and erasures, to enable the different and unique to emerge. Yet, as we've noted, postmodernism's own voice—the voice of critique—often sounds suspiciously universal itself. It is not only that it presents its own countertruths as truths. But also that, in doing so, it sometimes neglects to reflect on its own pedigree and perspective.

For instance, postmodernism often assumes a universal value of individuality and difference that might be accurate in Eurocentric cultures, but could be very different in, say, an Asian culture where the group is the primary social unit and group-belonging a primary social goal.

In addition, the ideas put forth sometimes seem unmarked for the very kinds of alterity they intend to promote, omitting considerations of age, class, sex, and race. We can see this in Foucault's much-repeated discussion of docile bodies, in which he analyzes disciplinary culture and the arrangement of architecture, time, and regimentation to instill norms that create a new form of power over individuals.

Yet it is reasonable to assume that racial minorities, women, transgender people, infants in nursery rooms, and retirees in rest homes all face very different regimes of discipline and are called to differing kinds of norms. In the same vein, when I wrote in an earlier chapter that "[this is] a fair description of the mechanics of gender in modern daily life. We are subject in daily life to a continuous dressage of gender," I appeared to be speaking a generalized truth in a universal voice, one that ignores that the mechanics in question may differ across lines of age, race, and class.

Is the sense of gendered subjectivity really the same for a 13-year-old girl as it is for a 73-year-old man? Are things like masculinity and queerness understood the same by black, Asian, and Native American males? Is the discourse on lesbian homosexuality really the same in the coal mines of West Virginia and the boardrooms of Wall Street?

In short, postmodern theorists sometimes seem to imagine a middle-class, middle-aged, Eurocentric version of Truth that they then faithfully deconstruct to make room for an alterity that their initial imaginings—located as they are in their own understanding of things—may have already left behind.

CONSIDERING RACE

This will only be remedied as writers step forward to wield deconstruction in ways that take such dimensions into account, particularly race. If the first truth of the body is its sex, the second is surely its race. And perhaps even vice versa: for race is the first thing we know for sure about bodies, and probably the very first thing we can see.

Yet gender and sexuality are understood as much more unstable and contestable than race. And deconstructing gender is accepted in a way that deconstructing race is not.

While someone might announce themselves to be a different gender or perhaps even a different sex and reasonably expect that proclamation to be respected, it is harder to imagine a symmetrical scenario if, say, someone with blond hair and big blue eyes announced he or she was an Inuit.

Have the politics of the raced body hardened or become off-limits in a way that the politics of the sexed body have not? Is race essentialized in a way that even sex is not? Or is it that more work has been done deconstructing sex than race?

If destabilizing notions of Truth is the price for a certain kind of freedom, is it possible to win a comparable kind of freedom when it comes to race? Is the pursuit of a new kind of discursive freedom in the face of racism relevant, or even moral?

If queer theory is primarily an inquiry into the truth of individuals and the questions about self-understanding they are called to answer, and if all of this is an integral part of what makes a racialist and racist system possible, then it is impossible for race to be exempt. Indeed, it may be morally indefensible to avoid the deconstruction of race. But if Foucault is right that nothing, including the body, is sufficient basis for self-recognition, let alone understanding others, then how are we to consider the raced body?

SHIFTING PERSPECTIVES

Such questions come at a time when the public debate on race is at a crossroads. Hispanic and Latina Americans have emerged as the most populous racial minority, while "new" minorities like

Arab-Americans are demanding increased recognition

Even as political positioning among traditionally recognized racial minorities is shifting, racial identity itself is undergoing a huge shift. In the 2000 census, when people were allowed to identify as "multiracial" for the first time, almost 7 million people—about 2.5% of the U.S. population—did so. With interracial marriage doubling in the last half-century and continuing to grow, Americans who identify as mixed-race are set to become perhaps the fastest growing racial minority of the 21st century.

A steadily increasing number of Americans are refusing traditional categories. Recall Tiger Woods' joking reply, when asked about his descent, that he was *Cablanasian*—Caucasian, Black, and Thai, plus (on his father's side) Native American.

Much of the new emphasis on multiracial identity originated in multiracial political groups' complaints that their identities were being made invisible. Meanwhile, traditional minority organizations fear that the splintering of racial identity is leading to decreased visibility (and political power) for *all* racial groups.

Despite these cultural trends, biologists continue to provide compelling new evidence of two basic facts: first, that racial distinctions have no firm basis in science; second, that every human being alive today is descended from the same (black) forbears who lived in a relatively small area in what is now called Africa. (Most languages—the primary marker of culture - that are spoken today seem to have come from another group of nonwhite forbearers who lived fairly recently in what is now Turkey.)

Race, it seems, may have more to do with culture than many people suspect. And questions about the reality of race are going to increase, especially as new theorists seek to expand deconstruction's reach beyond gender, sex, and desire.

WHAT IS RACE?

"In the late 19th century...it was not merely a historical coincidence that the classification of bodies as either 'homosexual' or 'heterosexual' emerged at the same time that the United States was aggressively constructing and policing the boundary between 'black' and 'white' bodies…"

Siobhan B. Somerville, *Queering the Color Line*

"The Western concept of sexuality…already contains racism…. The personality of the savage was developed as the Other of civilization and one of the first 'proofs' of this otherness was the nakedness of the savage, the visibility of its sex."

Kobena Mercer and Isaac Julien,
"Race, Sexual Politics, and Black Masculinity: A Dossier"
in *Male Order: Unwrapping Masculinity*

What is race? If it's not a matter of biology, something grounded in science and genetics, is it a matter of identification created by shared experience and cultural memory? And if this is so, how does such identity persevere when experience is lost or memory is severed?

As David Eng points out, identifying as Chinese-American seems to mean choosing between an Asian-ness located in old family memories from a country he's never seen, or one located in a combination of orientalist media stereotypes like Charlie Chan, Fu Manchu, Bruce Lee, and the hard-working, law-abiding "model minority" Asian immigrant.[7] And as Maxine Hong Kingston notes: "Chinese-Americans, when you try to understand what things in you are Chinese, how do you separate what is peculiar to childhood, to poverty, to insanities, one family, your mother who marked your growing with stories, from what is Chinese? What is Chinese tradition and what is the movies?"[8]

Wherever such writers turn, the specific Asian-Americanness they seek seems to recede, to be found somewhere else.

Maybe—as Beverly Tatum suggests in *Why Are All the Black Kids*

Sitting Together in the Cafeteria?—race is also based in binary opposition, in a sense of one's self as being whatever is *not* white, middle-class, mainstream, and therefore oppressive.

As white writers have noted, binary opposition also works in the reverse to create identity. whiteness *is* whiteness only to the extent that it is *not* blackness. Because the burden of being raced is borne only by minorities, the primary marker of being white actually becomes the absence of race. This absence is experienced through a freedom from having to recognize one's self *as* raced, or to develop a specifically racial subjectivity.

Perhaps race is at least as much a matter of identification as of politics. As some scholars have asserted, race may be simply whatever the dominant culture says it is, and whatever it needs it to be. This means that not only is race culturally constructed—but like gender or sexuality—it is constructed at specific times, in specific ways, in response to very specific needs that have little to do with the minorities being so constructed.

For instance, we used the U.S. Census to illustrate the shifting of racial categories and identities. Yet both the Census and the popular understanding it follows reflect a long and tormented history of changing direction when it comes to race.

Originally, most African-Americans were counted only as three fifths of a citizen. Hence, Jefferson was known as the "Negro president," because his margin of victory came from electoral votes garnered from slave-owners in Southern states who were casting their slaves proxies. To "protect" whiteness and ensure that mixed-race Americans remained subject to slavery, white America adopted the infamous "one drop" rule that held that any person with "one drop" of nonwhite blood was black.

Even today, both white and black Americans embrace this peculiar, overly broad definition, sustaining color distinctions that don't exist in other cultures. Meanwhile, the one-drop rule continues to cause what at least one writer has called "traumatic personal experiences, dilemmas of personal identity, misperceptions of the racial classification of well over a billion of the earth's people, conflicts in families and in the black community, and more."

By 1890, in the wake of slavery, the Census introduced separate categories for white, black, mulatto, quadroon, and octoroon, apparently in an effort to pin down with greater precision each nonwhite citizen's exact remove from white (which of course had no gradations). In 1920, these latter categories were recombined as simply black.

Yet once again, the needs of mainstream culture shifted. Waves of Anglo-European immigrants arrived via Ellis Island, and—although it may seem strange today—Irish and later Italian refugees were each considered black as well. Today, some Americans still consider Jewish to be a nonwhite racial designation, rather than a religion that includes everything from blue-eyed, red-haired native Israelis to black Ethiopians.

In 1977, the Census implemented four racial and one ethnic categories—American Indian or Alaskan Native, Asian or Pacific Islander, Black, White, and Hispanic Origin or Not of Hispanic Origin.[9] And today, the Census allows people to check multiple categories at will. Yet, for some scholars, this story does not so much chart a path of any progress as track how much and when the dominant culture needed certain kinds of racial distinctions.

Nor is the use of racial categorizations to preserve structures of privilege unique to white majorities or mainstream cultures. For instance, today both the Seminole and Cherokee tribes welcome predominantly white members seeking to reclaim their Indian heritage. But they continue to systematically reject predominantly black members who try to do the same thing, and thereby strip them of their right to tribal vote and energetically fight off claims to tribal benefits. (For more on this issues, see Brent Staples, "When Racial Discrimination Is Not Just Black and White," *The New York Times*, Sept 5, 2003)

GENDERING RACE/RACING GENDER

If there is no single basis for race, and if race is at least in part discursively constructed, then it must be inseparable from other dimensions like age, sex, class, sexual orientation, and gender. For instance, in a dialogue that exemplifies the complex connections among culture, class, and skin color, a raging debate is breaking out over exactly what Hispanic-American means, whether such a minority exists (apart from Anglo perceptions), and to whom it applies.

For some, Hispanic is a "slave name" that honors a powerful but predominantly white-skinned culture that originated in Spain and Portugal. This was a culture that invaded and colonized brown-skinned people of the Americas and the Caribbean for centuries. For others, the preferred name is Latina or Latino, recalling the predominantly South American heritage of the indigenous people that survived Hispanic aggression. And for still others, the preferred term is Chicana or Chicano—an identity that mobilizes a sometime term of derision and street slang that is being reclaimed as a sign of political and ethnic pride to describe Mexican and Mexican-Indian immigrants in the Southwest.

If race and class are so closely intertwined, gender cannot be far behind. Many writers who grapple with race and gender stereotypes treat them as separate entities. Yet as David Eng points out, racial ideals are seldom gender-neutral. For example, stereotypes of Asian women are inseparable from gender stereotypes of them as hyper-feminine, passive, and sexually exotic.

In a similar way, racial images of black "gangsta" males have mined gender stereotypes of hypermasculinity, emotional toughness, and sexual virility. Racist stereotypes of just this kind of primitive heterosexuality and predatory virility were mobilized well into the 20th century to justify lynching any black man who was even suspected of looking at a woman across the color line.

The flip side of this is the stereotypical white male, who might be a financially successful Wall Streeter and Yale graduate, but who from a gender standpoint is also bland, unaggressive, sexually uptight, and (need we say it?) rhythmically-challenged.

Perhaps all racial stereotypes are in some way implicit gender stereotypes, so that any understanding of how race is understood cannot proceed without also considering gender and even sexual orientation. The racial stereotype of the black thug is still impossible to think of as anything less than 100% heterosexual.

In the same way that the humility and docility of the Asian male stereotype is also a marker for orientation—for his absence of masculinity and virility generally, but his innate homosexuality specifically. As Richard Fung notes in *Looking for My Penis,* in the popular mind "Asian equals anus."

RETHINKING RACE

"[T]he answer to questions such as 'How should I act? What should I do?' [lies with] the peer group, the kids in the cafeteria, who hold the answers to these questions. They know how to be Black. They have absorbed the stereotypical images of Black youth in the popular culture and are reflecting those images in their self-presentation."

> Beverly Tatum, *Why Are All the Black Kids Sitting Together in the Cafeteria?*

"We are all borrowers and thus not pure…[I]dentity and identification never quite meet. All identifications are inevitably failed identifications."

> David Eng, *Racial Castration*

Perhaps there no racialness to be found in any racial stereotype, or even any racial identity, that is not intimately bound up with ideas of class, masculinity and femininity, straightness and gayness. So an analysis of race in isolation will always be incomplete. Perhaps the search for race after all is an illusion—there is no race to be found but the "dream of authenticity, the impossible quest for a pure self."[10] Thus white suburban boys call themselves "wiggers," and try to perform blackness, adopting the dress, masculinity, swagger, and style they see in urban black males.

At the same time middle-class suburban black youth worry that they are not black enough and may be derided as "Oreos"—just as young Asian-Americans or Native Americans who "act white" fear being labeled "bananas" or "apples," respectively.

From this perspective, one is not just one's race, one must learn *to be* one's race, even—in certain circumstances—to pass as one's race. As one teenager recounted, "'Oh, you sound White—you think you're White.' So ninth grade was sort of traumatic in that I started listening to rap music, which I really just don't like. [I said] I'm gonna be Black. My first year there was hell."[11] Is all minority identity a kind of learning, anchored not just in bodies and culture but in the process of imitation and the performance of who we're supposed to be? Just as one teenager learns to act black, another learns to butch it up or to act gay, while another learns to look real and pass as a woman.

Is all identity a kind of passing? In Eng's view, really being African-American or Asian or Chicano is very like being a Real Man or Woman—an approximation of an ideal that is always just outside one's Self. This sets up an impossibility that can never be perfect or perfectly coherent, a *doing* no more fully anchored by skin color than gender is by genitals. But if all this is true, then what about the un-raced race—white?

THE UNBEARABLE WHITENESS OF BEING

"[F]ollowing the Enlightenment, the encounter with non-whiteness would be framed in rationalistic terms—whiteness representing orderliness, rationality, and self-control, and nonwhiteness indicating chaos, irrationality, [and] violence...white racism and colonialism were morally justified around the conflation of whiteness and reason...[as] Foucault argued, reason is a form of disciplinary power.

Joe L. Kincheloe and Shirley R. Steinberg, "Addressing the Crisis of Whiteness," in *White Reign: Deploying Whiteness in America*

QUEER THEORY, GENDER THEORY

In mainstream American discourse, blackness has always stood for a kind of Other—the queer race—representing exoticism, primitiveness, and mysteriousness than enables whiteness to masquerade as the rational, the civilized, the known. In the oversimplified binary on race—recall that all binaries are by nature oversimplified—black performs for white a similar function as female does for male, or gay docs for straight. Femaleness or homosexuality emerge as odd, unnatural, and in need of explanation, enabling maleness and heterosexuality to be understood as normal, natural, and inevitable.

In *The Invention of Heterosexuality,* Jonathan Ned Katz began the deconstruction of straightness to give straight people the same kind of sexual orientation that gay people are necessarily so conscious of. Along the same lines, scholars in what is becoming known as Whiteness Studies have begun deconstructing what it means to white people to be white.

For instance, scholars such as Ruth Frankenberg listen to white people describe their experience of being white in a racially-charged world.[12] She finds in each person's inner experience a quiet awareness of *being* white that is built up through the small details of daily interactions, assumptions, and identifications.

In a sense, she and others are marking how white subjectivity is created from the bottom up, through the micro-politics of discourse. Such writers want to give white Americans the same sense of being raced that nonwhite Americans have historically been made to bear. They want to remove whiteness from its privileged position as the universal.

This is actually more difficult than it sounds, because of the way that privilege operates. It's easy to see discrimination when you're the target. But it's harder to see privilege, because privilege is basically defined by absence—the absence of discernable discrimination. And if privilege has been your consistent experience, you will tend to assume that your experience of the world—from being able to get a home loan to getting courteousness from shopkeepers to being able to hail a cab—is how the world normally operates. Racial discrimination will appear, not as a system, but as an aberration: dreadful to be sure, but nothing epidemic.

Whiteness Studies scholars seek to help white European people understand that racial discrimination is part of a *system,* and that racially intolerant acts are part of a different kind of normal life lived everyday by many Americans of color. Whiteness Studies tries to shift the focus from people of color as *disadvantaged* to understanding white people as *advantaged.* Its goal is to reframe the experience of normal as one that might in fact be specifically white and, we might add, specifically classed. For many of the privileges that are accorded to whites are also accorded based on class.

As Henry Louis Gates, Jr., and Cornel West observed in *The Future of the Race,* the difference between them and poorer blacks was much greater than the difference between them and their tenured white colleagues. Class amounted for as much of the variance as race.

In a similar fashion, many people assume that discrimination and violence caused by gender stereotypes are not big problems for most adults because they don't see a lot of it. This is because, once we're out of childhood, most of us eventually conform to gender norms.

But once you step *beyond the lines* in any profound way, you find a very different world, one in which a certain degree of confusion, scorn, and intolerance is the norm, and real "normal" seems a long way off indeed.

CRITICALLY RACED

We are at a point where the paradoxical goal of traditional liberal identity politics—a race-sensitive but color-blind meritocracy in which every person has a race but every race is equal—has begun to feel frayed. The liberal narrative of inevitable if incremental progress from within the system through law and activism is also looking shopworn. Although there have been some remarkable victories—particularly in the courts—racism remains an indelible part of the pattern of American society.

Over the last two decades, during what some are calling the

post–civil rights era, a new wave of writers, theorists and legal academics is rising to take the dialogue on race in new directions. These thinkers are equally dissatisfied with both liberal and traditional legal scholarship on one hand and the glacial pace of antiracist jurisprudence and legislation on the other

Proponents of critical race theory (CRT) are reimagining race and racial identity and their intersection with homosexuality and queerness. Motivating their work is the assertion that racialist— and even racist—behavior is not simply a cultural aberration but an important cultural norm. Therefore much of what constitutes racially discriminatory behavior will appear as ordinary. And going unremarked in discourse, it will thus also be unaddressed in law. Only the most egregious cases of discrimination will ever see the inside of a legislative chamber or a courtroom. The vast remainder of everyday racism that causes so much suffering and hurt will remain invisible.

Critical race theorists question core concepts of race by asking why race stratification exists, how it is applied, and how the institutions most charged with remedying its effects—law, religion, philosophy, and science—have contributed to its consolidation. Many of these writers constitute a second wave of progressive thought, wielding postmodernism to deconstruct yet another facet of bodies while correcting some of the omissions of the first.

By being willing to risk deconstructing the very identities they inhabit, they offer the hope of a new set of terms that might move the dialogue forward. Many, like Richard Delgado and Kimberle Crenshaw, come from legal backgrounds. They want to show that what the law regards as color-blind and normal in fact reflects a deep sense of white culture and implicitly mirrors white normality.

If law is based on the stories we tell ourselves as a society, then whose stories are these, and who is doing the telling and the listening? Is the growth of welfare rolls a consequence of the rampant incarceration of black males, or of "welfare queens" milking the system? Did O.J. kill his wife in a fit of jealous rage, or was he set up by the racist LAPD? Do Asian-Americans face significant barriers of racism, or does their apparent economic success prove that they are the "successful minority?"

Mainstream culture imagines law as a neutral arbiter that is above identities. Race-critical scholars see law and legislation as a series of stories the dominant culture tells itself to reflect and extend its own values and needs, but which maintains its power precisely by presenting itself as universal. This might include elevating the value of property above other social goods, vigorously punishing cocaine addicts but not alcoholics, or focusing on legislation to trim welfare rolls at the expense of laws that would increase employment. Much of the law assumes equal actors of equal privilege. But in a racist system, minority actors are almost never of equal status and privilege. Yet laws seldom take this into account.

CRT theorists try to "race the law," to make explicit the norms and narratives behind it, and promote alternative perspectives in their place. They use a wide variety of techniques—research, personal narrative, imaginary stories, and sub-subculture exploration—to reintroduce the context of minority lives into the dialogue, and thereby to return alterity into the discourse. In the words of Patricia Hill Collins, they want to shift "the controlling image."[13] Another way of saying this is that they are deconstructing the transparency of law and of legal language. By giving the law a raced perspective and history, they deny it a universal voice and the privileged position of pronouncing what is fair and just.

THE DEATH OF POLITICS?

But such efforts would seem to be politically dangerous as well, for in deconstructing identity, are such scholars not destroying the political base for actions. Feminist theorists have repeatedly warned that the death of Woman means the death of feminism, that feminist politics requires women in whose name feminist goals are pursued. In the same vein, doesn't deconstructing race mean denying the evils of racism—and the very reason for combating racism?

Yet CRT writers have increasingly shown that deconstructing racial identity need not mean the destruction of civil rights politics.

Rather, in Butler's terms, they seek to establish as political the very terms of emergence of racial identities.

The discourse of race is not just negative—restrictive and oppressive—but also productive. And as with gender and sexual orientation, the struggle against discrimination begins with asking how the dominant culture produces, enables, and demands a particular kind of person with a specific racial self-awareness.

CRT theorists' willingness to go "upstream" and ask how and why racial categories are produced shows that there need be no choice between racial constructedness and racial oppression. Nor does embracing such constructedness necessarily imply the denial of racial oppression.

Racial oppression is not just what happens to raced people, it is the how and why people emerge *as* raced. It is precisely because racial oppression is so persistent and painful that it becomes imperative to ask how power and discourse operate to produce raced bodies.

11. BUTLER AND THE PROBLEM OF IDENTITY

"[T]he identity categories often presumed to be foundational to feminist politics...in order to mobilize feminism as an identity politics, simultaneously work to limit...in advance the very cultural possibilities that feminism is supposed to open up."

"Laughter in the face of serious categories is indispensable to feminism."

Judith Butler, *Gender Trouble: Feminism and the Subversion of Identity*

THE PROBLEM OF IDENTITIES

What attracts us to many causes is the principle involved. You don't have to be a whale to join Greenpeace, and you don't need to be locked up in a foreign cell to support Amnesty International.

But when it comes to rights, we are attracted to the notion of identity—of rights for *us* as members of *our group*. Yet as theorist Judith Butler has shown, basing our politics on who belongs to which identity almost always leads to the same familiar set of problems.

Butler has questioned the traditional categories of identity—by gender, sex, sexual orientation, and race—that we use to navigate the traditional liberal narrative. In the process, she has reinvented much of feminist theory, becoming one of the founders of what has been named *queer theory.*

Her main tactic has been to refuse to accept identities at face value. She chooses instead to subvert them by asking such "upstream" questions as how they were created, what political ends they serve, what erasures have made them possible, and how they are able to present themselves as real, natural, and universal.

According to Butler, identity politics may have permanent problems. Because the concept of identity that underlies it—of *being* one's race or sex or sexual orientation—is itself seriously flawed.

She begins, strangely enough, with feminism. Feminism is understood as the movement that represents and pursues the political interests of women. What could be more straightforward than that? Yet, assuming a commonality to *any* identity, even one as apparently uncomplicated as Woman, can mean assuming a unity that doesn't exist in reality.

A political category called Woman may sound like a good idea in theory, but it hides immense racial, economic, gender, and cultural differences within it. Because of this, subpopulations within a common category may have very different political agendas. For instance, at one international women's conference, friction arose because American feminists were pushing an agenda focused on things like abortion rights and equal pay, while their Third World counterparts were pushing for an end to polygamy, female infanticide, female genital mutilation, and laws forbidding female property ownership.

Because it is unmarked for considerations like age, race, class, or nationality, the identity of Woman risks being—for political purposes, at least—more white, adult, middle-class, gender-normative, and Eurocentric than it should be.

The identity of Woman has also generated serious controversy over issues of ownership and identification. Some women have begun refusing the identity, particularly when it seems to draw—consciously or unconsciously—on middle-class, Eurocentric, feminine norms with the ironic effect that "women" are now opposing the unintended political effects of the very feminism working to liberate them.

Feminism has also faced conflict for just the opposite problem: refusing individuals who themselves identify as women and want to be represented by it. Stone butches, transsexual men and women, cross-dressers, intersexuals, queer youth, and drag people have all sought varying degrees of shelter and support under the banner of womanhood, only to be met with varying degrees of resistance.

This refusal itself generates additional problems. Not just the obvious one of correctly judging who should be allowed in, but the more subtle one of who is qualified to judge. For the very act of judging—regardless of who does it or what decisions they reach—creates a hierarchy in which some individuals are prelegitimated as women to judge those who follow. Liberatory movements should be about flattening hierarchies, not establishing new ones.

Yet the very act of judging itself assumes norms for acceptable womanhood and whose needs will really count. Once a hierarchy is in place, few who have been so judged will want to get involved, because no one wants to be a second-class citizen at their own party.

This is especially true with issues of gender, as mainstream feminism continues to either struggle with gender expression and identity or ignore these issues altogether, and young genderqueers—perhaps unaware that they are enacting a kind of fourth-wave feminism—turn away from mainstream feminism in droves.

This is the same problem we saw in other contexts with transgender organizations that are "also for anyone who is gender-different" or gay organizations that are "also for bisexuals." It's obvious who comes first, and thus who will actually come to play.

This problem cannot be resolved simply by saying, "Okay, then anyone can be a woman." If anyone can be a woman, then no one is a woman; the category loses any meaning. For it to retain any coherence, some people must inevitably be turned away. Feminism—a movement founded to counter the marginalization and erasure of women—ends up in the paradoxical position of installing its own margins and erasures.

Even worse, in the act of creating boundaries, feminism also creates its own limits. It risks creating a feminism that says to its young: Be all you can be, go wherever your heart and mind and talent can take you, but don't become too male-identified, too queer, or too masculine. If we can't recognize you as a Woman, we might not able to represent you within feminism any more.

In this way, according to Butler, a movement that embarks on the critical task of freeing women paradoxically also ends up imposing a new set of limits and restrictions on them. By refusing to analyze its own origins, feminism risks resembling that other universal monolith—patriarchy—that perpetuates its own dominance by asserting its naturalness, erasing whatever doesn't fit, and reimposing the Same.

STRENGTHENING THE BINARY

Upon further reflection, the problem may be even worse than it first appears. Feminism may have torn down many gender boundaries. But by unconsciously basing itself on binary genders, it has actually solidified structures like male/female, man/woman, and masculine/feminine in new and unexpected ways.

Woman turns out not only to be opposed to Man, but in some fundamental way—just as light requires dark—it actually produces binary notions of Man and Manhood. After all, what could it mean to be a Woman if not for Man and Masculinity? The terms are not only completely interdependent, like all binaries; moreover, they act to squeeze whatever doesn't fit, whatever "queers the binary," out of existence.

In this way, feminism has actually helped obscure the notion of gender transgression and the political aspirations of those who transcend gender norms by articulating its politics as if the whole world was divided neatly, naturally, into Boys and Girls. Similarly, the uncritical acceptance of gayness has reinforced the idea that an individual's sexuality ought to be the basis of his or her primary social identity, something unthinkable barely a century ago.

Meanwhile, gay activists have continued to fight for mainstream acceptance by pointedly comparing gayness to straightness—by arguing that gay people also are monogamous, raise families, and look gender-normal. While this has been politically effective, it has also made fidelity to sexual and romantic norms the basis for demanding social recognition.

Once again, difference is pushed aside. But as Butler points out, this is typical of power's uncanny ability to incite only those rebellions which—on a deeper level—are bound to fail because they unconsciously adopt and reenact the terms of their own construction.

FEMINIST REJOINDERS

Some feminists have tried to rebut these problems by reasserting a universal basis for Womanhood in women's common experience of patriarchal oppression. However, "the effort to identify the enemy as singular in form is a reverse-discourse instead of offering a different set of terms."[14]

In other words, just as feminists complain that patriarchy tries to reduce all women to a single narrow stereotype, so reducing patriarchy to a single narrow stereotype proves feminists can engage in the same tactic. Butler adds, "That the tactic can operate in feminist and antifeminist contexts alike suggests that feminism is capable of its own colonizing gestures."[15] Moreover, using male oppression as a unifying basis for womanhood renders Woman once again dependent on and derivative of Man. Even worse, it means that women are not defined by what they have become or what they have accomplished but rather by the sheer fact of their subjugation at the hands of men.

To avoid these difficulties, other theorists have tried to claim Woman as a strategic shorthand instead of a real identity. As a sort of temporary political position adopted for current political needs, it would not be expected to spell out its full meaning and complexity.

On one hand, temporary shortcuts for the sake of progress make sense. But they are also another kind of erasure, one that defers explaining all the messy, marginal subgroups that make up Woman in the name of political advancement. In fact, a goal of feminist advancement should be to recognize these marginalized components of Woman so that their experience is finally heard and acknowledged.

For the last couple of decades, so-called "radical" lesbian feminists have tried to perform an end run around all these problems. Refusing to debate any more nuanced notions, they have instead worked to construct a clear and specific definition of womanhood based on a specifically female embodiment.

Because of the way meaning is divided up in the gender binary, this embodiment has necessarily focused on those things that belong unarguably to the Feminine: motherhood, reproduction, and a distinctively female psychology that features empathy, nurturing, cooperation, sensitivity, and communicativeness.

The philosophical clarity of this view is refreshing. Such theorists have drawn a clear line in the sand for distinguishing "real" women from transsexuals, intersexuals, male-identified dykes, and others on the margins of identity.

Yet such "radical" essentialism has often seemed to come less from theoretical convictions than (as theorist Gayle Rubin has noted) a desire to make the offending messy realities disappear.

Which is to say, essentialist formulations often appear less like practices of identification than political formulas for legitimating exclusion. In any case, such essentialist arguments confound assertions that biology is not destiny or that one is not born a woman but rather becomes one. They require women to assume maternity and femininity as the essence of selfhood, in effect, reducing women to yet another stereotype, even if this time it is an entirely positive—or even "superior"—one.

Worse yet, a woman who fails to meet such standards—who does not yearn for the patter of little feet around the house; who is not nurturing, soft, or supportive; who revels in tough competition and in being an aloof, irritable loner—risks being written off as unfeminine or even male-identified. And she may be better off for it.

FEMINISM WITHOUT WOMAN?

The response to the arguments Butler raises isn't to ask feminism to completely refuse identities. In fact, it's likely that such a refusal is impossible, since discourse always carves up the political field into constituencies that will seek representation.

The answer is also not that the identity of Woman "simply needs to be filled in with various components of race, class, age, ethnicity, and sexuality"[16] so it can move forward in unity and conflict-free. The price of a less coercive feminism may be resigning ourselves to conflict and fragmentation and then agreeing to move forward with all our contradictions intact. Unities are boring, and a premature unity almost always means suppressing uniqueness, mobility, and difference.

As we saw with Foucault, identities are themselves the product of cultural constructions. If you begin identifying, tracking, and managing same-sex attractions, you eventually end up with a class of people understood as homosexuals. So perhaps it is not enough for feminism to simply fight for women's rights. Maybe part of a feminist agenda includes asking the "upstream" question of where the identity of Woman originated, how it is maintained, what hierarchies it creates, and whom these hierarchies serve.

Maybe, in addition to representing women, part of a feminist agenda should be questioning, even deconstructing the category itself, so that—paradoxically—feminism actually precludes a complete and final definition of Woman. In such a revitalized feminism, Woman is no longer assumed but is always incomplete and unstable, in the process of dissolving and reforming as the political needs emerge. And mobility of identity is no longer a threat, but an important tactic, even a central feminist goal, and the disruption of identity becomes a means to overturn the male/female, boy/girl, man/woman binaries that make patriarchy (and gender stereotypes) possible. The loss of unity and the incompleteness of the category might even promote new meanings, new ways of being, and new political possibilities for women to engage.

REIMAGINING GENDER IDENTIFICATION

A gendered identity is supposed to be an integral facet of "inner" personhood produced by one's biological sex. But there are problems with this. To begin with, what is the mechanism by which sex produces this inner identity? Where does the idea of interiority arise, and by what means "does the body figure on its surface the very invisibility of its hidden depth?"[17] And how does biological sex produce a gendered identity that invariably expresses itself into the same binary gender displays we inevitably see around us: dresses and high heels or suits and ties, pipe smoking or big hair and long nails?

For that matter, why do we understand the emergence of a proper gendered experience as a kind of achievement? Why does Aretha Franklin sing that her lover makes her feel "like a natural woman," or a soldier confide to his buddy that firing off a 50-caliber machine gun makes him feel like a real stud? Even our need to call attention to an especially authentic experience of gender by prefacing it with adjectives like *real* and *natural* illustrates how unconsciously aware we are that such states are psychological accomplishments.

And what can it mean to feel like a natural woman or a real man? Since these are binary opposites, one can only distinguish feeling like a real man to the exact degree that one does not feel like a real woman, and vice versa.

It appears that gendered identifications are only meaningful within a binary framework in which one term's separation from the other gives it meaning. Which points to a second problem: Each gendered identity must maintain a strict coherence among sex, gender identity, gender expression, and desire. Female is to woman as woman is to feminine as feminine is attracted to Male.

Breaking any link causes a gender to fall right off the grid of cultural intelligibility. Which is what happens to new formulations like bi-gendered cross-dresser, tryke (transsexual dyke), bio-boy (biological boy), andro (androgynous), butch bottom, or no-ho (no-hormone) tranny boy.

By breaking the links between gender, desire, and sex, they

become incomprehensible, idiosyncratic, a clever thing to do with words. What does gender identification mean if it doesn't tell us about a person's body, gender expression, and sexual orientation?

Yet since many combinations are available, how is it that only two intelligible genders are available? In fact, since we only become acceptable social actors by conforming to one of these two roles, maybe we should rethink the politics of gendered identification. Maybe our persistent sense of gendered personhood is actually an effect of gender instead of its origin. Maybe being a man or a woman is less the result of something we are than the result of regulatory practices of the gender system.

Perhaps "there is no gender identity behind the expressions of gender; that identity is...constituted by the very 'expressions' of gender that are said to be its results."[18] "Being" a gender is always a *doing*, a continuous approximation of normative ideals that live outside of us and were always already there before we arrived.

The shift in focus from the regulatory practices of the gender system to our inner "gendered identities" conceals gender's true origins beneath a substitute myth about nature, sex, and what is *inside of us*. Gendered identification is not an integral, independent feature of experience, but two accepted sets of meanings through which we are called to understand ourselves and to be understood by others.

As my friend Mariette once put it, "I know I am a woman, but a lot of the time, I don't feel like a woman. I don't feel particularly like anything at all. It's only when I put on a dress or a man looks at me that I really become conscious of it."

How, I wondered, is it possible to feel "like a woman?" Do all women feel alike? Does womanhood have a specific and universal kind of feeling? Is it a result of femininity, and if so, perhaps cross-dressers and drag queens feel "like women." Certainly, it is more than having a collection of female body parts.

Returning to Butler's notion of coherence, perhaps it is the authorization to understand and announce one's feeling of womanness, because one has the proper links among sex, gender, and desire. I suspect that many of us are like Mariette. Most of the time—whether we're brushing our teeth, driving the car, typing on our computer—we aren't conscious of any gendered identification at all. It is only when we're involved in a gendered act or situation that we feel like something specific, and then it's always one of two possibilities.

Because those are the only intelligible genders, the only ones that make sense. If the terms transgender male, boy-identified dyke, or intersexual female were available, maybe these would have been the identities with which we identified. For that matter, maybe these are the identities with which we identify, only we're unaware of it. If gender is a way to structure meaning, then we might easily be one of these genders and not know it, because—within our simplistic binary framework—they cannot exist.

In fact, why do any gender at all? What is the cultural demand that we answer to any gendered norm? Why can't Mariette simply feel like a woman when she does, feel like nothing at all when she doesn't, and have her little moments of masculinity if and when they emerge? Why can't she let all that be whatever it is?

GREAT PERFORMANCES

Butler believes that what we see as gender is performatively produced. This has been widely misinterpreted as "all gender is just a performance," something she not only didn't say but with which she very much disagrees. At a time when youth are increasingly aware of gender's elasticity and symbolic displays, when Hilary Swank wins an Oscar for playing Brandon Teena and Harvey Fierstein wins a Tony for playing *Hairspray*'s Edna Turnblad on Broadway, when college teens stage drag king parties, the notion of "gender as performance" is probably with us for good.

Performatives are the name for special kinds of speech that also qualify as official social acts. It sounds a little obscure, but consider that the words "I now pronounce you husband and wife"—when uttered by the right person at the right time before the right audience—create a marriage between a couple.

The words "I now pronounce you" do not comment *about* a marriage; rather, they *conduct* one. They do not just represent speech but also a specific kind of official social act. Such speech-acts are performatives, and we give them the power to do magical things.

For instance, a policeman who yells "you're under arrest!" at a fleeing suspect, or a woman who announces "I bet $1,000" in a poker game are not making descriptive statements *about* placing a suspect under arrest or making a bet. They are the acts of arresting someone and placing a bet themselves.

If I put on jeans, a tool belt, and hard hat, I don't really create the social state of my being a construction worker. I'm just referencing a particular style of dress associated with being a construction worker. But when I dress and act in a gendered way, when I pull on a dress and high heels and act in a recognizably feminine manner—when I *do* Woman—I am not simply referencing a gender role but constituting myself as one. I am creating the social state of being a woman.

This woman-ness is never there apart from my actions; I call it into being by creating it moment to moment. It has no more underlying identity or reality than being married, being under arrest, or making a bet. All of these exist only through a recognized set of acts that call into being important social states.

Unfortunately, performativity doesn't yet tell us a lot about why some performatives work and others don't—which with gender is a central issue. We want to know why some versions of *woman* or *man* work, while others fail.

For instance, I can do woman all I want, but I'm still going to be called "Sir" about half the time. And I have some butch friends who are very much involved in *not* doing woman, but who still get referred to as "Miss" (not to mention "Honey" or "Sweetie") about half the time. But the idea of performativity gives us hope that we might be able to reenact gender differently, to see genders that aren't *there* for us right now.

It reminds me of the parable of the anthropologist who goes in search of new genders. He sails to a remote, distant island, where the inhabitants recognize six of them. He goes ashore, and finds himself face-to-face with half a dozen statues representing gods, with one for each recognized gender. Crestfallen, the anthropologist turns around to continue his search elsewhere because, as he reports back, "like everyplace else, they had only two genders." Two genders were all he could see.

COPIES WITH NO ORIGINAL

The physical appearance of all males as men and all females as women is so compelling that it feels inevitable—a fact of Nature. Man and Woman look like the "real" genders. Anything else—male femininity, female masculinity, or something off the binary altogether—appears as a kind of gendered failure, bad copies, or knockoffs that didn't quite work.

For instance, drag works even though it shouldn't because we recognize its references as something real. When we see a drag queen, we may know the performer is not a woman, but we can't help seeing one because s/he stylizes her body in very specific, learned ways we recognize.

Yet the more we go looking for that real gender, the more it recedes and in its place, we find only other women, who also stylize their bodies in very specific, learned ways we recognize. Woman is to drag—not as Real is to Copy—but as Copy is to Copy. Gender turns out to be a copy for which there is no original. *All* gender is drag. All gender is queer.

Even the "real" genders are unstable and always changing. Think of Superman, the model of male masculinity. George Reeves, the original 1950s TV Superman, had a stomach that was larger than his chest, arms and legs that lacked any muscularity, a tochis built for two, and was clearly entering middle age. By comparison, his 1980s successor, actor Christopher Reeve, was the very embodiment of the young movie stud-muffin: taut, trim, youthful, and buffed-to-kill.

Butler finds the extraordinary energy we invest in embodying these moving, mutating, impossible heterosexual roles funny. "Indeed, I would offer heterosexuality as both a compulsory position and an intrinsic comedy, a constant parody of itself."[19] I would only add that the gay and transgender positions we try to embody are, in their own way, intrinsically comedic as well.

SEX INTO GENDER

Feminism has long stressed the separation between Sex and Gender to counter the assertion that women are defined by their ability to become pregnant and reproduce. Biology is destiny. Being female may be biological and thus unavoidable, but being a woman is cultural and therefore changeable.

From this perspective, gender is what culture makes of the sexed body. Put another way, "Sex is to nature or 'the raw' as gender is to culture or 'the cooked.'"[20] If gender is constructed, then Female need not become Woman. It could just as easily become Man, or something else entirely. And masculinity might become a property of Female as well as Male (or femininity a property of Male). In fact, if gender is what culture makes of sex, then even if sex is fixed and binary, there's no reason gender couldn't be multiple and variable.

Yet these things don't happen. Maybe if gender is what culture makes out of the raw material of sex, we need to ask exactly how that magical transformation occurs. Perhaps the distinction between sex and gender is not as useful as it first appears.

For one thing, if becoming a woman is an invariable result of being born female, then culture—not biology—is destiny. And all we've accomplished is to substitute one inevitability for another.

In addition, the sex-versus-gender distinction looks suspiciously like another return of the binary—and not only the obvious one of nature versus nurture. It also reenacts the more subtle binary of masculine versus feminine, in which the mute and passive body-as-feminine sits waiting, receptive and blank, for a vigorous and forceful culture-as-masculine to imprint it with meaning.

Once again the Feminine serves as Other, a tabula rasa to be appropriated for whatever meanings are necessary. Maybe the real problem is that there is no distinction between sex and gender. Maybe both are inevitabilities within a culture where reproduction becomes the central organizing principle for bodies.

Perhaps sex—the great, preexisting Given, the one immutable bodily fact upon which all deconstructionist arguments fail—is itself to some degree constructed. As we saw in the writings of Martin and Lacquer, although reproduction is a fact, what we make of it is heavily shaped by culture.

The weight of meaning accorded the male chest and female breast, the erect penis as potent and masculine, and the erect nipple or clitoris as feminine and vulnerable—all this seems less the result of a pristine Nature that lives out beyond culture than a construction that is culture's own product. An untouched and immaculate Nature turns out to be a very useful thing, successfully anchoring assertions about sex and bodies while inoculating them from all debate.

Yet Sex looks more like a gendered way of looking at bodies, of looking for and producing binary difference and then establishing it as the body's central organizing principle. We get a flavor of this gender-into-sex enterprise in over-the-top terms like opposite sexes, as if male and females were matter and antimatter.

Then Gender will not only be the meaning culture attaches to the sexed body, but the means by which and the reason that Sex itself is produced. Sex will be shown to have been Gender all along. The designation supposed to be most in the raw proves to have been already cooked, and the central distinction of the sex/gender narrative collapses.

POLITICAL POSSIBILITIES

If gender is constructed, what kinds of possibilities open up by virtue of its constructedness? If gender is a repeated doing that is always in danger of failing, what new political actions become possible?

This constructedness also allows for the possibility of subverting the gender an individual is *in* by embracing the failure, by failing publicly and purposefully and thus revealing gender's constructedness. The focus on individual subversive tactics reflects postmodernism's longstanding preference for private individual action. If enough people did it, it might indeed be a successful way to break down gender norms. But even if we accept the idea that a gendered identity is illusory or variable, many of us do gender as a way of expressing and communicating: "This is who I am. This is how I see myself. This is how I want *you* to see *me.*"

We understand gender as saying something important about us. We are not interested in subversion per se so much as a renewed sense of authenticity, of being all that we are, all of the time, without fear or shame or omission. For instance, when I fly, I'm often addressed loudly and repeatedly as "Sir" by airport security personnel who are busily wanding my breasts. I console myself with the reminder that this is what subversion looks like.

This confusion over pronouns and genders used to make me feel ashamed, as if I was a personal failure. But then one day I was shopping and ended up going from the men's shoes to women's lingerie to men's socks. Every salesperson, every department, fumbled for pronouns. All of them were unsure how to treat me. (Was I looking for men's shoes for myself or shopping for my boyfriend? Was I a lady buying underwear or a pervert pawing through women's underthings?)

I remember asking myself, Why should everyone be able to tell instantly on sight whether I'm a man or woman? Doesn't that reenact the central tyranny of the gender system—that we must fit ourselves into these little boxes so people can always tell what we are at a glance?

Maybe all the social discomfort and confusion I was causing— not to mention my shopping spree's zigzagging across gender lines— was the price for a certain kind of freedom. Maybe it was the price of something new. Maybe in the face of all the gender restrictions we must confront, *new* feels like anxiety, social awkwardness, and even tension as people try to figure out something that makes them suddenly unsure.

For myself, I realized I was not so much interested in parody, but in—as my partner likes to put it—"using all my voices." If being "who we are" is off the gender binary and therefore appears to parody and therefore subvert gender roles, then we might embrace subversion. But otherwise it's unclear whether subversion per se has much of a future as a sustainable political practice.

If her solutions have not yet been totally embraced, Butler's ideas have nonetheless generated enormous enthusiasm among students, academics, youth, and activists. In the end, the question that hangs over Butler's brilliant, unruly philosophical campaign is the one with which she herself introduces her first book: What shape of politics emerges when identity no longer constrains our politics?

At present, postmodernism is unable to tell us why we should care about the shape we have or why we should desire a different one. It's more than a little like Scarlet O'Hara promising breathlessly that "tomorrow…is another day," without knowing that tomorrow will be better or even explaining why it should be.

In this sense, postmodernism seems to trade on the assurance that newness itself is filled with enough promise. And it is this hopefulness that I think postmodernism trades in (even if unintentionally).

There is an increasing sense among people interested in liberation movements that the traditional progressive narrative is stuck. As befits a broad coalition of groups and identities, we are concerned with issues of inclusion and difference.

At the same time, particularly in the case of gay rights, we sometimes risk becoming obsessed with making sure no one is left out of or unnamed in our lesbian, gay, bisexual, transgender, intersexual, queer, questioning, straight-sympathetic allies youth movement—otherwise known as the LGBTIQQSSAY.

And identities, which once promised such pride and freedom, have sometimes looked like overly simplistic labels that submerge our individuality and erase more complex intersections with factors like age, race, and class. In addition, the emphasis on difference and identity has produced a loose mosaic of differing agendas brought together by necessity rather than a strong coalition of shared values that engages in effective political action.

Finally, youth are emerging with a new vision that sees narrow, fixed identities as confining and unnecessary. Young folks embrace nonbinary genders and multiracial identities with equal facility.

It's time for the next step, which is what postmodernism and the possibility of postidentity politics offers. When Butler impertinently demurs from the idea of writing for a gay anthology as a lesbian, because the name announces a set of terms she wants to contest, we sense that something new and unexpected is in the offing.

With gender, as with politics, there is also this feeling of being stuck. Thirty years of feminism and gay rights have convinced many of us that there is something deeply wrong with gender roles, yet gender seems as compelling and inevitable as ever. We look around, and all we ever see are men and women and nothing else.

So for me, Butler's primary value was to help me to see that this was not inevitable—that there were cracks in the system. These openings could be used to introduce change—to allow me the space to believe that seeing men and women on every corner didn't mean either that they were there or that I necessarily had to become one.

This sounds simple enough, but for me, ideas like these represented enormous personal breakthroughs, and they were the main reason I buried myself in gender theory. Yet despite gender theory's popularity on college campuses, it has also remained largely a creature of academia—obscure, complex, and abstract. While it undoubtedly offers new tools to "open up the discourse," can that be translated into organized politic action?

12. GENDERPAC AND GENDER RIGHTS

I've tried to use this book to offer the theoretical tool set that helped me answer questions about what I was or wasn't, or why I didn't conform to gender stereotypes. This tool set also helped me to start organizing like-minded people to end the discrimination and violence caused by the gender stereotypes I saw all around me.

And it is all around: in the restricted way we raise our children, in bullying at school, in workplace terminations and public ridicule and gender-based assaults. As I write this, a teenager has been stabbed to death in Newark, N.J. Sakia Gunn looked like a handsome young African American boy. According to her mother, she was dressed "like a boy" when a car pulled alongside her early this morning at 3 A.M. She was only 15.

None of the news reports mentioned rage toward Sakia's gender nonconformity as a possible motive for the assault. If we don't talk about hate crimes like these, we can't stop them from happening again.

This final chapter is where all the theory has been leading. For me, it's what this whole book has been about. Gender stereotypes cause real, profound, and pervasive social suffering and hardship. The suffering is no less real because we don't always see the issue. It's time we organized to stop it. It's time we put theory into action.

BEGINNINGS

Women's rights, gay rights, and transgender rights had all taken big bites out of the apple of gender stereotyping. In 1995, the time was ripe for a national organization to focus directly and exclusively on achieving gender rights.

This was the idea behind my founding the Gender Public Advocacy Coalition or GenderPAC. What was true then remains true today: The people most interested in issues of primary identity— of gender expression and identity—are those most often identified with them. I'm talking about transgender people.

Transpeople are still the only community who will readily identify the problems around gender. Almost everyone else is too ashamed to do so, or chooses to reinterpret issues with the gender system through sex or sexual orientation.

But for transpeople, having issues with gender is the basis for common identity. Transpeople have no choice but to attack gender norms, because their very existence is in itself a challenge to gender norms, no matter how well they might visually conform to them,.

GenderPAC was formed to be a gender rights group, but its roots are in the transgender community. By early 1996, several directors began envisioning GenderPAC as the national transgender political organization, while I was committed to the vision of an organization pursuing the principle of gender rights for all.

This contradiction placed it squarely on a political fault line, and predictably the very first fight we had was over who owned GenderPAC and gender rights. There was a short, fierce struggle behind the scenes over a period of months. No work was done. All the energy anyone had went into this fight. Barely a year old, the organization was already on the verge of breaking apart under the pressure of competing visions and competing political agendas.

On one hand, other national organizations almost completely ignored GenderPAC—the acronym LGBT had not yet been widely accepted—and there was a deep need for a national transgender political group.

There still is. Because the community is very small and geographically dispersed, often fractious, and composed of multiple subgroups, it has been hard to build national political organizations from scratch. At the same time, gay organizations have amassed money, infrastructure, and political legitimacy.

Thus, the transgender community has always been torn between building its own institutions to represent its own interests, and leveraging the muscle of the gay rights movement by demanding greater inclusion of transgender people. As of this writing, most transgender activists appear to have come down firmly in favor of the latter.

On the other hand, it was difficult for transgender activists who were loudly trumpeting the virtues of inclusiveness to gay groups to demand an exclusive transgender-focused group for themselves. In the end several organizations left the board, and a number of new groups—gay, bisexual, and intersex—were invited to join. We went forward with at least a nominal commitment to the ideal of inclusion and the principle of gender rights for all, but the problem was far from over.

In addition to our political troubles, we had money troubles. We had hardly grown; in fact, some years we had virtually no budget and had to depend on a handful of volunteers for nearly everything. While I talked about gender rights, because we lacked the money and resources to create programs, in reality we could only respond to events, and of course all the events we were asked to respond to involved transsexuals.

Wherever I spoke, everyone seemed to understand that when I said "gender rights for all" what I meant in practice was "transsexual rights for us." In any case, people couldn't seem to hear what I was saying over the sound of my body.

We were talking the inclusive talk but walking the transsexual walk. It was the best of both worlds: look radical, play to the base. I was aware of the contradiction, but I had so much to do and so few resources that I thought the situation would resolve itself .

TIME TO WALK THE WALK

Later came much sooner than expected, in the form of our first full-time employee, Managing Director Gina Reiss. I might have been good at public speaking, theory, and "the vision thing," but I had no formal organizational skills or professional experience as an activist. Gina, on the other hand, was the real deal.

All she had ever wanted to do was activism, and she'd waited tables at night so she could learn her profession. Starting as a volunteer, she worked her way up to become action vice-president of NOW-NJ. Next, she headed the New Jersey Lesbian and Gay Coalition as its first executive director, and went on to help found the Federation of Statewide LGBT Advocacy Organizations together with veteran leaders such as Urvashi Vaid, the former executive director of the National Gay and Lesbian Task Force.

Gina had a genius for organization and a penchant for working long hours. Animated, intense, and frighteningly assertive, she did not suffer fools gladly. With dark, slender good looks, she looked like a striking gay-boy just exiting his teens whom you might see shopping at Banana Republic.

She was looking for a way to connect her lesbian and feminist politics with the fact that she was frequently the target of all manner of gender harassment, from men in the street to women who pulled her bodily out of restrooms. She seemed to find some of that connection in our message, and in 1999 I asked her to come aboard. She reluctantly agreed to try the job for a couple of months, unsure that GenderPAC was about people like her.

Her first act was to organize our first real fund-raiser. She somehow managed to get Hilary Swank, who had just won an Oscar for *Boys Don't Cry*, and the film's director, Kimberly Peirce, and things took off from there.

Gina brought us two things. First, she put a formal organization under my rhetoric, installing a member and donor program, a formal accounting system, a fund-raising structure, a grant application calendar, an annual conference, and our first real board of individuals.

Second, she began consistently challenging me on why—if we were really were a gender rights group—everything we worked on was based on transsexuals, with nothing on gays, lesbians, feminists, minorities, straight Americans, or youth. (She quoted my own books when arguing with me, a particularly unpleasant tactic.)

It was not that I was being duplicitous or obtuse. It was just that every story that came in the e-mail, every legal case involving gender had to do with transsexuals. The reason for this is both simple and profound and has to do with the problem of trying to shift paradigms: There are no gender cases except transgender cases. There is no gender news that is not transgender news. There is no gender lawsuit that is not a transgender lawsuit. There is no gender-inclusive legislation that is not transgender-inclusive legislation.

People simply do not have a box in their heads labeled "gender rights." Everything that is not transgender falls into a different box: gay, feminist, or something else. For instance, when Sakia Gunn was stabbed to death in Newark, the newspapers and the groups that commented on the murder identified it as a "gay hate crime," even though she looked like a young African-American boy, and her mother noted that she and her friend were "dressed like boys." Gender disappears.

Similarly, when legislation was introduced in New York City to protect the right to gender identity and expression, *The New York Times* and local progressive groups hailed it as "transgender legislation." When people saw *Boys Don't Cry*, they saw a "transgender movie," but when they saw *Billy Elliot*, they didn't see a "gender movie" but simply a film about a boy who loves to dance. And when 38-year-old African-American bus driver Willie Houston was shot to death in Nashville by a man who became enraged to see him holding his fiancée's purse, no one identified it as gender-based violence.

A top official at one of the country's largest gay organizations, an executive with millions of dollars and for whom at least a half-dozen butch lesbians work, recently told me that his group would like to talk more about gender violence and gays, "but we don't have those cases." No one knows about gender-related cases because no one sees gender-related cases. Attacks against gay people, because of their gender expression, go into a box labeled "gay hate crimes." Discrimination against women because of their gender expression goes into a box labeled "sex discrimination."

Even when *The New York Times* carried a front-page article on the epidemic of male-on-male gender harassment in the workplace, it didn't use the words "gender rights." The only things that go into the boxed labeled "gender" are those that involve transsexuals.

A BOX CALLED GENDER EQUALITY

Since we couldn't look for gender-related news, we began a tedious process of reading gender *into* the news. We would analyze lawsuits, legislation, and hate crimes to look for gender stereotypes.

And did we find them!—gay men who were attacked because they were, or were perceived as, effeminate; a class-action suit by female employees who were kept in traditionally "feminine" jobs; boys who were beaten up for liking pencils and math more than girls and sports; girls who were ostracized for being mouthy, aggressive, and too athletic; grown women with massive medical problems because as little girls they had been treated with megadoses of estrogen so they wouldn't grow "too tall." Gender-related problems were all around. We just had to look through a different lens.

Moreover, as we began to draw attention to these cases, it became apparent that everyone was at least vaguely aware of them or cases like them I've never been in front of any group—gay or straight, young or old, men or women—where someone says, "Oh, I don't think this is a problem at all." Everyone gets that gender stereotypes are a serious social problem. They just don't understand combating them as a logical extension of the civil rights movement...yet. It's like a revolution of the obvious.

But that's our job. By reexamining news, law, art, and politics, we at GenderPAC were able to greatly expand our work, our membership, our foundation, and corporate support. In the process, we precipitated the second great crisis that once again almost brought GenderPAC down.

FULFILLING OUR MISSION

As one of our directors pointed out, no matter what our mission statement said, GenderPAC had functioned as the de facto political head of the transgender community. Was it fair to widen our work when there were "limited resources" for nontransgender people?

Some directors had begun treating Gina and other board members as if they were allies who were there to assist the transgender-identified people who "really" had a problem with gender. The volume of this disagreement grew louder and louder. Our internal listserv went radioactive; one director asked to be taken off it and another simply resigned from the board.

When things finally came to a head, one group of directors declared that women had NOW, gays had HRC, and transpeople should have GenderPAC. Another group—the staff and the interns held to the wider vision of GenderPAC as a gender rights organization for all Americans.

In the end, either we were a gender rights group for all, or we were the political voice of the transgender community. Each was a good and necessary thing, but there was no way to bridge the gap and be both things at once.

Something had to give, and it did. Three transgender-identified directors quit in a highly emotional and public break. With them went two gay-identified directors who were disappointed to find they were not, after all, on the board of a transgender organization.

The national transgender magazine devoted most of its next issue to attacking me personally, and hate e-mail—much of it particularly personal—began showing up in our in-box on a daily basis. In a fit of unintended irony, a national gay organization that had recently added transgender to its mission, took to the editorial pages of the *Washington Blade* to attack GenderPAC for being insufficiently transgender in focus.

The country's largest transgender conference withdrew a grant they'd awarded us, declaring that the same inclusive vision that they'd applauded when awarding it was—now that we were actually fulfilling it—a betrayal of the transgender community.

Gay organizations, worried that they would antagonize their transgender constituents, began distancing themselves from Gender-PAC. Other groups that had been working with us to fulfill their transgender quotient found themselves in the new and unfamiliar position of actually having to do some work on transgender issues.

Coalitions suddenly had to start looking for a new group to fill the T in their LGBT. Some activists simply sat on the sidelines, wondering what in the world GenderPAC could be if it wasn't the national transgender group. A national gay organization, one I'd picketed in a different incarnation because they weren't transgender-inclusive, responded to a suggestion of joint action by saying that they "first have to check with some people in the transgender community."

And in a delicious turnaround, transgender leaders invited other groups to a Capitol Hill meeting on key legislation—something we had been working on for a decade—but excluded GenderPAC on the grounds that it was "not a gay or transgender group."

All the chickens had come home to roost. Old complaints by gay activists that scarce resources shouldn't be wasted on nongay concerns were replaced by new complaints by transgender activists that scarce resources shouldn't be wasted on nontransgender concerns.

Many of the activists who were loudest in attacking us for being too inclusive (*too* inclusive?) were the same ones who relentlessly attacked gay organizations for not being inclusive enough. This proves, I guess, that inclusion and diversity are good things, as long as it's someone else that has to do the including.

Identity politics has bequeathed us the unwieldy notion that exclusion is okay, but only if it's done by a minority group or one whose oppression ranks higher on the totem pole of pain. Thus a whites-only group is unacceptable, but a blacks-only one is not. A gay-but-not-transgender group is offensive, but a transgender-only one makes perfect sense.

WHO OWNS GENDER RIGHTS?

For myself, I believed a gender rights movement that left trans-people behind was a failure. But a movement that aspired to help transgender people without mounting a sustained attack on the way the gender system oppresses each of us—especially children—was a failure too.

Gender rights must become something more than this stepchild of gay rights and feminism that is identified solely by the right to transition from one sex the other. I know the sound of laughter at your back. I know the sound of your wife-girlfriend-lover closing the door behind her. I know the pain of not being able to see immediate family members or nephews, nieces, and cousins.

I know how much it hurts to hear your own parents say they're not sure they can bear to see you again. I know what it's like to be in a strange and hostile place and mourn someone you've never met, and I know what it's like to be kicked out of your job and your home.

I have heard about similar experiences from feminists; gays and lesbians; minority genderqueer youth; artistic, chubby, asthmatic little boys beaten up in locker rooms and tough, athletic, little straight girls who've been ridiculed and bullied. All have paid a price for transgressing and transcending gender norms.

The importance of gender oppression, whatever our identities, is that we understand how the gender system works. We've seen the moving parts behind the curtain. We have our hands around an ageless and yet transformative truth—one that is so obvious that no one sees it yet. But it is a secret that hides in plain sight, and if we don't do this work, if we don't mount this movement, who will?

Most of us don't get paid to fight our battles. We're citizen activists—the most beleaguered and sometimes the most lonely kind. We work to improve the world because at heart we're still naive, still romantics. If we're sarcastic or jaded, it's not because we've lost our love for full equality, but because we've been disappointed in that love.

Even in this age of political cynicism, we believe things can be better, that we each deserve the right to be fully and openly all that we are. We live in a time of balkanization, not a melting pot but a checkerboard. We're gay or straight, Democrat or Republican, conservative or liberal. We work for women's rights, gay rights, Latina/o rights, Jewish rights, transgender rights, youth rights—whoever constitutes "us."

We don't work for anyone else's cause, because what would be the point? It's a black thing, a gay thing, a transgender thing, or a woman thing: You wouldn't understand. And we wouldn't be welcome anyway. Better stick to your own.

Our presidents say "my fellow Americans," but we know they don't mean it anymore. They really mean "my base and all the crossover votes I need to get reelected." Even our progressive organizations seldom speak to the best in us anymore; they seldom offer a vision that demands more of us than the enlightened self-interest of pursuing equality for ourselves. There is a power in naming one's self, being with one's own kind, of breaking into smaller and more homogenous groups. But I am still troubled about making identity the main foundation of our politics.

As we splinter into finer and finer groups, it may be that even if I am wrong, the centrifugal forces of identity politics may have flung us far enough out into our own orbits that it's time to start looking for common issues that bring us together. Gender is one of those issues. Gender rights are too fundamental to belong to any one group and too important to leave anyone behind. Gender rights are human rights, and they are for all of us.

CAN BUTLER WORK?

Butler poses tempting questions about the political possibilities that emerge when identity no longer constrains our politics. She points to promising new possibilities for organizing that bring us together in new and unfamiliar ways.

While she holds out the promise of something new, Butler has also tended to constrain her actual suggestions for political actions to parodic repetitions of leftist imperatives to subvert the existing order from within.

If this is not edifying stuff, it is in keeping with postmodern cynicism toward the possibility of "liberation" (there is no way outside of discourse) and its tendency to equate community and organized groups with tyranny. Butler seems to restrict the possibilities for political response to isolated individual acts of insubordination. But I don't believe that will be enough.

It is likely that gender equality will require new laws, attitudes, and civil rights. Changing courts, legislatures, media coverage, and public opinion will require not only individual subversions of the gender system but also the mobilization of people into organizations and movements.

Yet no one has any idea how to apply gender theory here, or how it works in "the real world." No one has had to answer the question: What kinds of organization and mobilization are possible once identity no longer constrains our politics?

In my work I've tried to take some ideas from gender theory generally and Butler specifically and then apply them to political activism. As I wrote in the introduction to this book, postmodernism should not be just theory but also applied science. In that spirit, I'll offer some of those ideas below.

The first is simply that gender is a legitimate human rights issue, even though it may not yet be recognized as such. It requires not only civil rights–like laws, government policies, and judicial verdicts, but also something more like social rights—the right to be you without fear, or shame, or omission.

For me to realize that took lots of reading, theory, and study. I spent about three years talking and thinking about not much else. But you don't need all that theory to get there. You just need to realize that people shouldn't be pushed from birth into these two funny little boxes called boy and girl, or be punished when they don't fit neatly into either box.

How should we organize to achieve such rights? To begin with, I think we need to recognize that Butler is on to something when she says that identity politics may be permanently troubled. No matter where the boundaries of identity are drawn, a hierarchy is inevitably created in which some people who want in are kept out, some people who want out are pulled in, and some people have more legitimacy than others because they happen to personify the identity norms.

This is especially problematic for a gender rights movement because it is supposed to be about the right to more authentically express your gender. If we start pushing people back into a normative straight-jacket from the get-go, why bother?

Gender rights are for everyone, regardless of how they identify. It would no more morally right for GenderPAC to refuse to help someone because they weren't transgender than it would be to refuse to help them because they were. If we believe inclusion is a good thing for others, then it must be a good thing for us as well. Movements and organizations become stronger when they welcome people as members instead of as allies. Welcoming someone as merely an ally can betray a mindset that "this isn't really your problem, but you're welcome to help us."

At some point we need to get beyond questions of how people identify or whether they count as us and return to our advocacy for guiding principles that can apply to anyone who needs them.

Saying that gender stereotypes hurt everyone is not the same thing as saying that it hurts us the same way. We need to allow for individual difference. Moreover, we need to remember that people are always more complex than the movements that seek to represent them. We need to look further for the intersections in people's lives. It's not enough to say, "It's all gender, honey." Because it isn't all gender. It's gender and race, or gender and class, or gender and sexual orientation. People face multiple challenges, and although our issue may be simple, their lives and bodies seldom are.

Watch for those struggling at our own margins, and strive to bring them into the center of our own work. No matter how hard we try to be inclusive, the thrust of our work will invariably create centers as well as margins where some people will be sidelined.

We must be aware of who is not in the room, who is alone, and whose voice is not being heard. We need to be aware of the effects of our own discourse and remedy them wherever possible by bringing our margins back into the center.

Encourage what is different and unique. The thrust of our politics should not be to make everyone the same, but to help people be different—to make it safe and acceptable for them to be different.

Civil rights will not be enough; we need social rights as well. Gender-based oppression is not only or primarily accomplished through the power of the state: police, courts, and laws. It's also accomplished through peer pressure, shame, ridicule, and ostracism. To make it possible for people to transcend gender lines, we must not only change laws and policies, we need to change social attitudes and raise awareness of gender harassment.

Conforming to gender roles—becoming a recognizable boy or girl—may be the founding social act. (An infant that is still an "it" is not a real social actor yet.)

Gender rights is an unfamiliar issue, and almost everything about gender transgression is surrounded by shame and discomfort for many people. To bring them into our movement, we will need to work with everyone's level of comfort.

Finally, it's not easy to get people from different constituencies and communities to work together. Identities empower us, but they also separate us from one another. So work to bring people together.

GENDERPAC

The Gender Public Advocacy Coalition (GenderPAC) works to end discrimination and violence caused by gender stereotypes by changing public attitudes, educating elected officials, and expanding legal rights. To get an idea of just how broad and how urgent that vision is, consider that in just the last two years:

* Russian-American New York athlete Aaron Vays, age 12, was hospitalized by bullies who warned him "only girls and sissies" figure-skate. Two-thirds of respondents to an ongoing GenderPAC School

Violence Survey reported being harassed or attacked because of their nonconformist gender expression or identity.

* At Harrah's casino in Reno, Nevada, 44-year-old feminist Darlene Jespersen was allegedly fired after more than 20 years when she refused to wear makeup under a new dress code. Meanwhile, in New York City, 32-year-old lesbian Dawn Dawson was allegedly fired for looking "too butch." In New Orleans, truck driver Peter Oiler was terminated after two decades on the job when he admitted to his manager that he occasionally cross-dressed at home.

* *The New York Times* has reported that male-on-male sexual harassment now accounts for nearly one-in-seven new claims filed at the Equal Employment Opportunity Commission, much of it related to gender stereotypes. According to the EEOC, many of these are male employees who find themselves targeted for harassment for being insufficiently aggressive or because superiors considered them too effeminate.

* Six teens of color have been murdered in gender-based attacks, including African-Americans Ukea Davis (18, District of Columbia); Stephanie Thomas (19, District of Columbia); Nikki Nicholson (19, Michigan); Sakia Gunn (15, New Jersey); Latina student Gwen Araujo (17, California); and Native American Fred Martinez Jr. (17, Colorado).

From classrooms to boardrooms, from reservations to the city streets, transcending narrow gender norms can get you harassed, assaulted, or killed. Change won't come quickly; this struggle is just beginning. But now more than ever, GenderPAC is committed to making gender rights a reality. Our work programs focus on Community Violence Prevention, Workplace Fairness, and Gender and Youth. One step at a time, with help from activists in local communities around the country, these programs have produced real results. In just the last year:

* Our Workplace Fairness Program has helped educate corporations such as IBM, J.P. Morgan Chase & Co., Kodak, Proctor & Gamble,

and Verizon on adopting or implementing new EEO policies that protect employees' rights to gender expression and identity.

* Our Community Violence Prevention program has held events in over two dozen local communities—featuring speakers such as Pauline Mitchell (the mother of Fred Martinez, Jr.) to educate people on gender-based hate crimes.

* On Capitol Hill, in a new partnership with the Human Rights Campaign (HRC), we've persuaded 76 Members of Congress—including five Republicans and eight Senators—to sign a new diversity statement that adds sexual orientation and gender identity and expression to the hiring policies covering federal legislative staff members.

* Our recent National Conference on Gender (featuring a keynote address by Judith Butler!) drew 1,500 activists from 36 states, 72 student groups, and 74 organizations for three days of events.

There is so much work that remains to be done if we're to have gender rights. But with each step, GenderPAC comes closer to the goals of safer communities, fairer workplaces, and schools where all children are valued and respected. Our newest effort is the unique GenderYOUTH Network. Developed by leading youth activists, GenderYOUTH is a national network that supports college leaders in mobilizing their own campus GenderROOTS chapters.

Chapter activists launch their own initiatives and campaigns to raise gender awareness and combat gender-based bullying and violence on campus and in local high schools though peer-to-peer outreach, grassroots organization, and community education. College activists have responded with enthusiasm. At Gender-YOUTH's formal roll-out at the National Conference on Gender in May 2003, college groups launched the first 14 chapters.

The next step GenderPAC is researching is a parental support network. If you're a parent who wants to raise a child who's not boxed into one gender stereotype or the other, there's very little support out there. Things such as educational materials, a Web site, and networks of like-minded, supportive parents could go a long way toward helping people parent more organically self-actualized and sane children.

What is so exciting about gender rights work at this historical moment is that doors that have been shut for decades are finally springing open. Ten years ago no state or municipality had laws protecting their citizens' right to gender expression and identity. Now more than 60 do, including cities such as Tucson, Arizona; Springfield, Illinois; Louisville, Kentucky.; El Paso, Texas; and Toledo, Ohio, and also the states of Minnesota, Rhode Island, and—just this March—New Mexico. Similar legislation is pending in Illinois and Texas.

A decade ago no major corporation protected employees' right to gender expression and identity in the workplace. Now 18 do, including blue-chip companies such as American Airlines (the first ever to do so), Apple, Nike, and Intel. Dozens more are planning to do likewise.

A few years ago, almost no company was interested in expanding their EEO policies to include gender rights. Few corporations understood the issue or were comfortable with it. To many, it seemed a little obscure or even weird. Few followed up with us after an initial contact. Today, companies are reaching out to us for language, background, support, and on-site staff training. Gender-rights talk is not merely welcome; companies realize it's the new edge of "best practice" in the workplace. And if they want to remain leaders in diversity, they need to be among the first to develop this practice.

But with new rights have come new dangers. A dozen years ago, a hate-based crime might have involved a white 30-year-old post-operative transsexual who had gone on the wrong date with the wrong guy. Today, it's more likely to be a teenager of color, often from an economically challenged home, who is gay, of indeterminate gender, experimenting with gender roles, or transgender—but not necessarily transsexual. The victim's assailant is likely to be another youth.

When I was in secondary school, it would have been unthinkable to show up in a dress. The boys' football team would have reduced me to a small spot on the locker-room floor. Today, youth are doing more radical and complicated things with gender at younger ages than we ever could have anticipated.

In fact, not a month goes by without someone—youth or adult—who has been taunted, harassed, fired or assaulted reaching out for help.

GenderPAC is working hard to grow as quickly as we can to meet the challenge. Four year ago our budget hardly existed, and we were a small group of volunteers. Today, we have an office, staff, members, a growing donor program, and expanding corporate and foundation support. We're growing by about 30% a year.

This is what change looks like when it happens. This is what a new paradigm looks like when it starts to take off.

This is a movement whose time has come. Join us. If you've read this far in the book, it's an issue that speaks to you too. Don't let gender rights stay "just theory." Get involved. Because gender rights are human rights, and the time for them is now.

NOTES

1. Michel Foucault, "Two Lectures," in Power/Knowledge: Selected Interviews and Other Writings, 1972-1977 (New York: Pantheon Books, 1980) p. 98.

2. Michel Foucault, *The History of Sexuality: An Introduction* (New York: Random House, 1990) p. 43.

3. Del Martin, *Lesbian/Woman,* revised edition (New York: Bantam Books, 1983), p. 49

4. Nancy Fraser, *Unruly Practices: Power, Discourse and Gender in Contemporary Social Theory* (Minneapolis: University of Minnesota Press, 1989) p. 44.

5. Kathy Russell, Midge Wilson, and Ronald Hall, eds., *The Color Complex: The Politics of Skin Color Among African-Americans,* reprint edition (New York: Anchor Books, 1993) p. 66.

6. Thomas Laqueur, *Making Sex: Body and Gender from the Greeks to Freud* (Cambridge, Mass.: Harvard University Press, 1992) p. 153.

7. David Eng, *Racial Castration: Managing Masculinity in America* (Durham, N.C.: Duke University Press, 2001) p. 17-27.

8. Ibid.

9. Siobhan B. Somerville, *Queering the Color Line: Race and the Invention of Homosexuality in America* (Durham, N.C.: Duke University Press, 2000) p. 169.

10. Eng, *Racial Castration,* p. 25.

11. Beverly Daniel Tatum, *Why Are All the Black Kids Sitting Together in the Cafeteria? And Other Conversations About Race,* 5th edition (New York: Basic Books, 2003) p. 60.

12. Ruth Frankenberg, *White Women, Race Matters: The Social Construction of Whiteness* (Minneapolis: University of Minnesota Press, 1993) p. 47.

13. Patricia Hill Collins, *Black Feminist Thought: Knowledge, Consciousness, and the Politics of Empowerment,* 2nd edition (New York: Routledge, 2000) p. 103.

14. Judith Butler, *Gender Trouble: Feminism and the Subversion of Identity* (New York: Routledge, 1990) p.13.

15. Ibid.

16. Ibid., p. 15.

17. Ibid., p. 134.

18. Ibid., p. 25.

19. Ibid., p. 122.

20. Ibid., p. 37.

INDEX

INDEX

butch/femme(s) 11, 14, 26, 99
Butler, Judith 82, 83, 86, 103,
    121, 123, 126, 127, 129, 131,
    132, 134, 139, 150, 151, 155

Capitol Hill 14
Catholic Church 41
—and sexuality 49-51
Census, U. S. 64, 112, 113
—2000 Census 110
"Centers" 152, 153
Chase & Co. 154
Chase, Cheryl 72, 73, 75-81,
Cherokee 113
Chicana/o 114, 116
children, genderqueer 60
Chinese American 111
civil right(s) 153
—black 5
civil rights movement 5, 146
Class 114, 118
clitoridectomies 82, *see also* IGM
CNN 9, 35
Collins, Patricia Hill 120
Communist 13
Community Violence
Prevention Program 155
conservative(s), social
conservatives 6, 7, 9, 13, 16,
    17
—Republican 14
"construction of sexuality" 52
Crenshaw, Kimberle 119
Critical Race Theory,
    Theorist(s), (CRT) 84, 121

—defined 119
—law and legislation 120
cross-dresser(s), cross-
    dressing 11, 22, 23, 26,
    27, 28, 37, 39, 51, 53, 60,
    61, 99, 125, 131
—bi-gendered 130
—conventions 22, 23
—and sexual pleasure 28
—in transgender movement 27

Davis, Ukea 154
Dawson, Dawn 154
deconstruction, deconstructing
    101, 109, 136
—"culturally constructed" 44
—defined 44
—gender 109
—identity of Woman 129
—race 109, 120
—sex 84-86, 109
Delgado, Richard 119
Derrida, Jacques 33, 34, 35,
    38, 39, 40, 42, 43, 44, 45,
    48, 62, 99, 103
—Critique as process 99
—politicizing thought 98
"different but equal" 8
discourse 71, 75, 97, 99, 104,
    117, 119, 129, 139, 153
—academic/feminist 60
—defined 59
—limitations of 69, 98
—medical/psychiatric 60
—on gender 59, 60

INDEX

INDEX

—American 5
—fourth-wave 125
—lesbian 17
—mainstream 125
feminist(s) 6, 7, 10, 19, 28, 44,
    127, 128, 144, 145
—academics 61
—theorists 99, 120
—theory 106, 124
—mainstream 11
femme 39, *see also*
    butch/femme
fetishistic transvestitism 60
Fierstein, Harvey 132
Foucault, Michel 1, 47, 48, 51,
    53, 57, 59, 68, 69, 71, 74, 89,
    95, 98, 101, 102, 103, 107,
    108, 129
—construction of sexuality 52
—as homosexual 49
—politicizing knowledge 98
—on prisons 65-67
—self as constructed 48
—and "self-knowledge" 47
Fox News 35
Frankenberg, Ruth 117
Fraser, Nancy 63
FTMs (female-to-male
    transsexuals) 10, 28, 30

gametes 87-88
Gates, Henry Louis Jr. 118
gay(s) 13, 15, 22, 25, 26, 29,
    72, 104, 135, 143, 145
—activists 14, 16

—boys 37
—effeminate 14
—groups 143
—hate crimes 146
—in the military 14
—movement 5, 15, 29, 143
—rights 9, 13, 106, 142
—theory 106
"gaze of the jailer" 67
Gearhart, John 75
gender 2, 11, 15, 16, 17, 18,
    20, 36, 59, 69, 93, 102, 109
—activism 19
—based violence 145
—conformity 69
—as constructed 44, 135, 136
—deconstruction of 109
—defined 35
—discourse on 59
—as "a doing" 39, 131, 136,
    137
—as drag 134
—dysphoria 60
—equality 151
—expression 8, 19, 125
    130, 131,142, 145, 146,
    156,
—as gay issue 17
—harassment, male-on-male
    28
—as human right issue 151
—identity, identification 8, 26,
    125, 130, 131, 132, 145
—intolerance 19
—issues 18

INDEX

INDEX

INDEX

man, male 40, 126, 128, 134, 135, 135
—femininity 134
—male-identified dykes 128
"mannish" women 7, 16, 37
Marable, Manning 107
Martin, Emily 87
Martinez, Fred Jr. 154
masculine 8, 9, 15, 38
—symbols 15
masculinity 4, 6, 7, 8, 15, 37, 65, 97, 115, 126, 135
masochists 53
Mattachine Society 13
McGowan, John 33
menstrual blood 93
menstruation 88
Mercer, Kobena 111
meta-narrative 5, 33
Michigan Womyn's Music Festival 30
Millet, Kate 99, 100
misogyny 11
Mitchell, Pauline 155
mixed-race 110, 112
modernism 33-35
Ms. Foundation 20
mulatto 113
multicultural curricula 102

National Coming Out Day 51
National Conference on Gender 155
National Day of Remembrance 24

National Gender Lobby Day 25
National Organization of Women, NOW 10, 11, 147
NOW-NJ 144
Native Americans 116
Navratilova, Martina 86
"nellie" fairies 18
New Jersey Lesbian and Gay Coalition 144
New Republic 35
New York Times 9, 28, 35, 145, 146, 154
Newsweek 9
National Gay and Lesbian Task Force (NGLTF) 24, 144
Nicholson, Nikki 154
Nike 25, 156
no-ho tranny boys (no-hormones) 39, 130
Nussbaum, Martha 101
NYPD 14

octoroon 113
Oiler, Peter 154
"one drop" rule 84, 112
"one-sex" model 90-94
"opposite sexes" 86
ovaries 92

Pathy Allen, Mariette 131, 132
patriarchy 45, 99, 100, 126, 127, 129
performatives, performativity 132-133

[167]

INDEX